Detours

LESSONS FROM JOSEPH

The Unpredictable Path to Your Destiny

TONY EVANS

LifeWay Press®
Nashville, Tennessee

Published by LifeWay Press® • © 2016 Tony Evans • Reprinted 2017

ISBN 978-1-4300-5534-1 • Item 006104401

Dewey decimal classification: 234.9
Subject headings: CHANGE (PSYCHOLOGY) \ FATE AND FATALISM \ PREDESTINATION

Scripture quotations are taken from the New American Standard Bible®, Copyright © 1960, 1962, 1963, 1968, 1971, 1972, 1973, 1975, 1977, 1995 by The Lockman Foundation. Used by permission. (lockman.org)

To order additional copies of this resource, write to LifeWay Resources Customer Service; One LifeWay Plaza; Nashville, TN 37234-0113; fax 615-251-5933; call toll free 800-458-2772; order online at lifeway.com; email orderentry@lifeway.com; or visit the LifeWay Christian Store serving you.

Printed in the United States of America

Groups Ministry Publishing • LifeWay Resources • One LifeWay Plaza • Nashville, TN 37234-0152

Contents

About the Author

DR. TONY EVANS is one of America's most respected leaders in evangelical circles. He is a pastor, a best-selling author, and a frequent speaker at Bible conferences and seminars throughout the nation.

Dr. Evans has served as the senior pastor of Oak Cliff Bible Fellowship for more than 35 years, witnessing its growth from 10 people in 1976 to more than 9,000 congregants with more than one hundred ministries.

Dr. Evans also serves as the president of The Urban Alternative, a national ministry that seeks to bring about spiritual renewal in America through the church. His daily radio broadcast, "The Alternative with Dr. Tony Evans," can be heard on nearly one thousand radio outlets throughout the United States and in more than one hundred countries.

Dr. Evans has authored more than 50 books, including *Oneness Embraced*, *The Kingdom Agenda*, *Marriage Matters*, *Kingdom Man*, *Victory in Spiritual Warfare*, *The Power of God's Names*, *God's Unlikely Path to Success*, and *Horizontal Jesus*. Dr. Evans, a former chaplain for the NFL Dallas Cowboys, is currently the chaplain for the NBA's Dallas Mavericks, a team he has served for more than 30 years.

Through his local church and national ministry, Dr. Evans has set in motion a kingdom-agenda philosophy of ministry that teaches God's comprehensive rule over every area of life, as demonstrated through the individual, family, church, and society.

Dr. Evans is married to Lois, his wife and ministry partner of more than 40 years. They are the proud parents of four—Chrystal, Priscilla, Anthony Jr., and Jonathan.

Introduction

I don't know about you, but I like to get to where I am going without any detours. When I take a long road trip with the family, I won't even stop for normal things like food and bathroom breaks, unless my family insists. So you can imagine how I feel about a detour. It's not good. I sigh. I moan. I wonder why on earth did this have to happen to me right now.

Few of us like to be stalled, for any reason. But detours are necessary if any improvement is going to be made on the paths we travel, or if any wreck is going to be cleaned up or hazard avoided. Detours are designed for our own good, regardless of how we view or feel about them. Detours are a good thing that often feel bad.

As people, we like to plan. We make our itineraries when we travel. Or we keep a log of our schedule on a calendar app. We appreciate the efficiency of moving forward steadily. We would never plan chaos and detours into our lives on purpose. And yet that seems to be God's *modus operandi*—His go-to mode for guiding us.

Rarely does God ever take someone to the destiny He has for them without taking them on a detour, or two or ten, or even a hundred.

Not too long ago, one of the men from the church came over to my home to meet with me. He had been going through a rough time. As he sat in my family room, head hung low, he lifted his eyes to mine and said, "Pastor, I feel as if my detour has met another detour and they got married and had a baby detour." In other words, he felt as he were running into detour after detour after detour and that the detours merely kept replicating and multiplying rather than taking him anywhere meaningful.

God will take us on a detour because He is constructing something in our lives as well. Granted, detours are anything but convenient. They take you out of the way. They are longer than you originally had planned to travel. But they are necessary. God is more interested in your development than your arrival. He cares more for your character than your comfort, more for your purity than your productivity.

How we view our detours will often determine how useful they wind up being. Which is why we are going to spend the next few weeks examining the purpose, power, and perfection of the detours God both uses and allows in our lives.

How to Get the Most From this Study

This Bible study book includes six weeks of content for group and personal study.

Group Sessions

Regardless of what day of the week your group meets, each week of content begins with the group session. Each group session uses the following format to facilitate simple yet meaningful interaction among group members, with God's Word, and with the teaching of Dr. Evans.

START This page includes questions to get the conversation started and to introduce the video segment.

WATCH This page includes key points from Dr. Evans's teaching, along with blanks for taking notes as participants watch the video.

RESPOND This page includes questions and statements that guide the group to respond to Dr. Evans's video teaching and to relevant Bible passages.

Personal Study

Each week provides five days of Bible study and learning activities for individual engagement between group sessions. The personal study revisits stories, Scriptures, and themes Dr. Evans introduced in the videos so that participants can understand and apply them on a personal level. The days are numbered 1–5 to provide personal reading and activities for each day of the week, leaving two days off to worship with your church family and to meet as a small group. If your group meets on the same day as your worship gathering, use the extra day to reflect on what God is teaching you and to practice putting the biblical principles into action.

Tips For Leading a Small Group

Prayerfully Prepare

Prepare for each meeting by—

REVIEWING the weekly material and group questions ahead of time;
PRAYING for each person in the group.

Ask the Holy Spirit to work through you and the group discussion as you point to Jesus each week through God's Word.

Minimize Distractions

Create a comfortable environment. If group members are uncomfortable, they'll be distracted and therefore not engaged in the group experience. Plan ahead by taking into consideration—
SEATING;
TEMPERATURE;
LIGHTING;
FOOD OR DRINK;
SURROUNDING NOISE;
GENERAL CLEANLINESS
(put away pets if meeting in a home).

At best, thoughtfulness and hospitality show guests and group members they're welcome and valued in whatever environment you choose to gather. At worst, people may never notice your effort, but they're also not distracted. Do everything in your ability to help people focus on what's most important: connecting with God, with the Bible, and with one another.

Include Others

Your goal is to foster a community in which people are welcome just as they are but encouraged to grow spiritually. Always be aware of opportunities to—
INCLUDE any people who visit the group;
INVITE new people to join your group.

An inexpensive way to make first-time guests feel welcome or to invite someone to get involved is to give them their own copies of this Bible study book.

Encourage Discussion

A good small-group experience has the following characteristics.

EVERYONE PARTICIPATES. Encourage everyone to ask questions, share responses, or read aloud.

NO ONE DOMINATES—NOT EVEN THE LEADER. Be sure that your time speaking as a leader takes up less than half of your time together as a group. Politely guide discussion if anyone dominates.

NOBODY IS RUSHED THROUGH QUESTIONS. Don't feel that a moment of silence is a bad thing. People often need time to think about their responses to questions they've just heard or to gain courage to share what God is stirring in their hearts.

INPUT IS AFFIRMED AND FOLLOWED UP. Make sure you point out something true or helpful in a response. Don't just move on. Build community with follow-up questions, asking how other people have experienced similar things or how a truth has shaped their understanding of God and the scripture you're studying. People are less likely to speak up if they fear that you don't actually want to hear their answers or that you're looking for only a certain answer.

GOD AND HIS WORD ARE CENTRAL. Opinions and experiences can be helpful, but God has given us the truth. Trust God's Word to be the authority and God's Spirit to work in people's lives. You can't change anyone, but God can. Continually point people to the Word and to active steps of faith.

Keep Connecting

Think of ways to connect with group members during the week. Participation during the group session is always improved when members spend time connecting with one another outside the group sessions. The more people are comfortable with and involved in one another's lives, the more they'll look forward to being together. When people move beyond being friendly to truly being friends who form a community, they come to each session eager to engage instead of merely attending.

Encourage group members with thoughts, commitments, or questions from the session by connecting through—

EMAILS;
TEXTS;
SOCIAL MEDIA.

When possible, build deeper friendships by planning or spontaneously inviting group members to join you outside your regularly scheduled group time for—

MEALS;
FUN ACTIVITIES;
PROJECTS AROUND YOUR HOME, CHURCH, OR COMMUNITY..

Week 1

THE PURPOSE OF
DETOURS

Start

Welcome to session 1 of Detours. Begin by taking a few minutes to be sure everyone knows one another, especially if this is your first time meeting as a group.

When has your life been going one direction and then something happened to make it change course?

When a detour occurs in your life, how have you generally reacted toward it?

Dr. Evans describes a detour as an unexpected shift in the route we were trying to travel. We often think of detours that happen when we are in our cars, but Dr. Evans will explore the detours of our lives and how the Lord sends them and uses them to draw us closer to Him.

Before we learn what Dr. Evans has to teach us about detours, would somebody pray for our time together, asking the Lord to open our hearts and minds to His Word as we begin this study?

Watch

Complete this viewer guide as you watch the video for session 1.

A _Detours_ is an unplanned, often unexpected, _Shift_ in the route we were taking to get to where we were trying to go.

Detours are determined by:

1. _Testing_ _Diasters_
2. _Training_ _Desire_
3. _Temptations_ _Developement_

Your destiny is your divinely-designed _____ .

Joseph was given the position of the _____ .

Why does God not take us on a direct route from where we are to where He wants us to be?

1. To _Test_ us

   A _Test_ in the Bible is an _adverse_ _____ that God causes or allows to take place in our lives to bring us to the next level of _spiritual_ _Development_ .

2. To _TRAIN_ us

   Detours have a way of _exposing_ you to things that you were unaware of previously for the purpose of _TRAINing_ you.

3. To _Prepare_ us

In order for us to be tempted, it may come from Satan, but it must be _Allowed_ from God. _Temption_ proves whether you are _Ready_ for what God wants to give you.

Our destiny is all about keeping _Close_ _Proximity_ with God.

Respond

Discuss the video with your group, using the questions below.

How do you think of detours when youencounter them while driving?

How do you normally feel when your plans run into detours?

Do you ever take into consideration the purpose of a detour? Does that influence how you respond or react to the detour?

Dr. Evans discussed three reasons why God uses detours. How have you seen these three reasons for detours brought about changes in your life?

Dr. Evans said, "A test in the Bible is an adverse circumstance that God causes or allows to take place in our lives to bring us to the next level of spiritual development." How have you seen testing grow or change you spiritually?

Have you ever tried to refuse taking a detour? What happened as a result?

When you have been on a detour, what are some important lessons you learned along the way?

Share some biblical examples of God leading someone in a "roundabout way" toward an intended destination.

What are some emotions you commonly feel when you're stuck taking long detours?

Read James 1:2-4. What does James say our perspective should be on "detours"?

Read week 1 and complete the activities before the next group session.

Positive Interruptions

When we get in our cars, we do so with a destination in mind. We plan to go somewhere. We typically know how we plan to get there, which highway we are going to take—even which streets we are going to turn onto in order to arrive at our destination.

And if we don't, we at least type in the destination address into our smartphone app and rely on an automated voice to guide us every step of the way.

Whether we are following our own mental map or the one in our phone, sometimes we run into a detour—some closed end that requires us to make a U-turn or go down a path we had not previously expected.

I don't know about you, but I like to get to where I am going without any detours. When I take a long road trip with the family, I won't even stop for normal things like food and bathroom breaks, unless my family insists, so you can imagine how I feel about a detour. It's not good. I sigh. I moan. I wonder why on earth did this have to happen to me right now.

Have you ever done something similar? You can admit it, too.

Few of us like to be stalled for any reason, even if it's just someone cutting us off in traffic and forcing us to slow down. But detours are necessary if any improvement is going to be made on the paths we travel or if any wreck is going to be cleaned up or hazard avoided. Detours are designed for our own good, regardless of how we view or feel about them.

They are a good thing that often feels bad.

Divinely designed detours in our lives are also positive interruptions designed to divert us to a better path so that we might have the opportunity to reach our destination well. What's more, they often provide the development we need in order to reach our destiny. How we view our detours will often determine how useful they wind up being, which is why we are going to spend the next few weeks examining the purpose, power, and perfection of the detours God both uses and allows in our lives.

Day 1
THE ROUNDABOUT WAY

Few of us like to be stalled for any reason, even if it's just someone cutting us off in traffic and forcing us to slow down. But detours are necessary if any improvement is going to be made on the paths we travel or if any wreck is going to be cleaned up or hazard avoided. Detours are designed for our own good, regardless of how we view or feel about them.

Detours are a good thing that often feel bad.

If you were to sit at a detour sign and stubbornly refuse to take the diversion, you would go nowhere. You would just sit there. For days. Possibly weeks sometimes. Yes, a detour may cause you to take longer than you had originally planned; however, it won't take any longer than if you were to try to push through it on your original path. That will get you nowhere.

Ultimately, while detours may feel like negative things, they are good things. They provide safety, opportunities for road improvement, and a different way to get you where you wanted to go. When viewed from a short-term perspective, they may not seem that good, but when you look at them from at the overall long-term vantage point, they are always good. This is why your perspective toward personal detours matter and will influence the impact they have on your life. If you spend your time complaining rather than seeking to understand the purpose of detours, you will be less likely to benefit from them.

Share how you feel when you come across a detour while you are driving. Do you ever take into consideration the purpose of the detour, and does that influence your emotions at that moment?

In what ways might understanding that your personal detours have a purpose (as opposed to those you come upon while driving) affect the way you view them?

As people, we like to plan. We make our itineraries when we travel or keep a log of our schedule on a calendar app. We appreciate the efficiency of moving forward steadily. We would never plan chaos and detours into our lives on purpose. And yet that seems to be God's modus operandi—His go-to mode for guiding us.

Rarely does God ever take someone to the destiny He has for them without taking them on a detour, or two or ten, or even a hundred. It is the one-in-a-million Christian who gets to go from point A to B to C and straight on to Z. Most often God takes you from A to F to D to R to B to Q and so on. You never know which letter He is pulling out next, either.

> **Read Exodus 13:17,18. Why did God not allow the Israelites fleeing Egypt to take the shortest, straightest path?**

> **The New Living Translation records Exodus 13:18 like this, "So God led them in a roundabout way through the wilderness toward the Red Sea." Give another biblical example of God leading someone in a "roundabout way" toward the intended destination.**

> **Share a personal example of how God led you in a "roundabout way" toward a desired goal. What are some important lessons you learned on the path?**

God has a plan for you. He has a plan for your life. He has a purpose for your existence. The reason why you were not taken to heaven the moment after you were converted is because you have a purpose on earth He desires you to live out. Your destiny is not just to go through the motions day in and day out. It is a God-designed stamp on your soul that involves the use of your time, talents and treasures for His glory, for good, and for the advancement of His kingdom.

Yet, the development of your talents, the increase in your treasures, and the wisdom you acquire doesn't always come quickly. Just as an Olympic athlete must train day in and day out in order to prepare himself or herself for the race, or event, we are on a path to destiny that requires development.

Read Habakkuk 2:3. What are we to do when what we have been shown or guided to do faces a delay?

Wait patiently. and watch.

Is God mean to make us wait? Why or why not? *No - He is preparing us for a service that only I can do!!*

List three benefits you can gain from delays in reaching your destiny or purpose in life.

1. *Development of specific set.*

2. *Patients makes to reward sweeter*

3. *Delay keeps me from injury, myself or others*

God is a loving Father. His heart desires for you to be all that you can and should be. But just as any parent would not put their five-year-old child in high school, God knows that we require time and lessons to develop us to reach our destiny.

Thus, part of experiencing the fullness of your destiny simply comes in understanding your detours.

Far too often, we fail to understand our detours, and as a result, we wind up viewing them in a wrong light. When this happens, we give room for things like impatience, bitterness, regret, and doubt to grow. Rather than allowing the detours to produce the development we need, they actually set us back spiritually, setting us up with a need for more detours in order to grow. It can become a vicious cycle.

What are some common emotions and reactions we feel when our "plans" run into a detour?

Anger, frustration, anxiety, Hurt

Read Psalm 37:5. What does it mean to "commit your way to the Lord"? Can you simultaneously hold on to "your way" and "commit" it to God? Why or why not?

What are the benefits of committing your life path to God and trusting in Him? Also read Proverbs 16:3.

If you've never made the connection between your detours and your destiny, will you take some time to intentionally look at your detours in this light? It might be helpful to rehearse past detours in your life by writing in a journal or on a notes app and recording how these detours were used to get you where you are today.

Prayer

Heavenly Father, thank You for these lessons on detours and how You use them to positively impact my life. Please open my eyes to see how You have done this in my past and even how You are presently doing this in the circumstances and situations I face. I want to approach life's detours in a mature manner so that I don't cause additional delays. Increase my wisdom, patience, and insight so that I can. In Christ's name, amen.

Day 2

THE IMPORTANCE OF DEVELOPMENT

When you were in school you had to take regular tests. These tests let the teacher know where you stood on the material you needed to learn. If you didn't pass those tests, then more assignments and more tests would have needed to be given.

Have you ever known someone who "tested out" of a class or an assignment? Have you ever done this? What enables a person to "test out" of a class or assignment?

What prevents someone from testing out of a class or assignment?

God is not going to bring you to the fruition of your destiny until He knows you are able to handle it spiritually, emotionally, physically, and the like. If you cannot handle it, you will lose it rather than use it for His glory. That is why He focuses so intently on our development as He takes us to our destiny.

The timing and length of our detours in life are often dependent upon our personal choices and growth. God may have a short detour planned for us, but we make it longer through our hard headedness, stubbornness, resentment, or immaturity and doubt.

What things can make a detour longer? Have any of these things ever made your detour, and what did you learn from that experience?

For those of you who work out, did you know that your muscles change almost immediately after a strength training session? The process called protein synthesis occurs anywhere from two to four hours after exercising. This is how the muscles grow stronger and bigger. Even though it happens so quickly after strength training, it is typically four to six weeks before noticeable muscle changes are seen by others.

Have you ever started an exercise regime only to quit it because you did not see any results? If so, how long after starting did you quit?

Why is it important to continue exercising even when you do not see immediate results?

How can we apply this physical lesson to our spiritual and personal lives with regard to the development we are experiencing in our detours?

Can you list three practical ways to remind yourself to keep going in those times when you do not see any results? Be sure to use scriptural truth to back up these reminders when possible.

1.

2.

3.

Moses was on a detour for forty years. He knew what God wanted him to do. God wanted him to deliver His people from slavery. Yet it took forty years in the wilderness to develop Moses into the humble and trusting servant that he needed to be in order to have the mindset, faith, and abilities to carry out the plan.

Abraham was on a twenty-five-year detour. At one point God had told him His plan for him—that He would bless nations through Abraham and make his name great. The vision and the proclamation from God to Abraham were real and vivid. It would have been odd for Abraham to believe at that point that it would be nearly three decades before he would witness the literal birth of it. But it was.

The greatest apostle in the New Testament, Paul, went on a three-year detour to a desert where God removed him from the front page of culture and life in order to strengthen him, teach him, and develop him for his calling.

Detours are often a regular part of God's plan in guiding us to our destinies. God will often give us a glimpse of our destiny long before we are prepared to actualize it, as He did when He told Abraham that there would be a 400-year detour in Egypt before they would reach their promised destination (Gen. 15:12-16).

Read Acts 24:24-27. In your own words, describe the situation that Paul faced.

How might Paul have felt, languishing in jail for so long?

Do delays always come with a ready explanation? Why or why not?

Read Psalm 62:1 and Psalm 69:3. List some common emotions that come when we are waiting on God, stuck in a detour we do not understand.

What are some common feelings experienced when someone exercises longer than they want to or more frequently than they want to due to doctor's orders, the encouragement of others, or even personal willpower?

Share some approaches to overcoming the desire to give up when negative emotions appear and to push through even when results are not readily apparent.

Have you ever had to do this in your own life? Describe the situation and the ultimate result.

Development is not an event. Neither is it a one-size-fits-all experience.

Development takes time, tests, failure, and overcoming. God knows each one of us individually. He knows what we each need in order to develop and strengthen our spiritual muscles and sharpen our spiritual insight and wisdom. More often than not, this requires detours in life to allow us the opportunity to learn, grow, and develop.

God has a destiny for you. He has a purpose and a plan that He wants you to live out. But it may not happen tomorrow. You probably won't get there by going in a straight line. Patience is a preeminent virtue needed in order to reach your destiny.

Read Romans 5:3-5 out loud. Substitute the word "detours" for the word "tribulation" or "affliction."

Hope does not disappoint. Detours disappoint, momentarily. But when we allow them to produce hope, God promises that hope will not disappoint. But in order to arrive at an authentic hope in your spirit, accepting your detours is necessary.

Just like your muscles will not grow simply by wishing them to grow stronger, neither will your hope The process of strengthening your hope comes by detours, tribulations, afflictions, and trials.

Show me someone with an <u>indomitable</u> hope, and I will show you someone who has had his or her share of detours. This is because authentic hope is a learned trait. Authentic hope is that level of hope which stays steady despite the storm and circumstances. It is the hope that enables you to keep going on faith alone.

impossible to subdue or Defeat.

Prayer

Loving Heavenly Father, thank You for your gift of detours.
Thank You for loving me enough to want me to grow, develop,
and mature. Thank You for not giving me my destiny or dream
too soon, before I am able to handle it because then, Lord, I may
waste it, lose it, or even ruin it. God, You know what is best.
And You are a gracious Lord to patiently develop me to reach
that place of ultimate purpose and destiny. I am thanking You
in advance for all You have in mind. In Christ's name, amen.

Day 3

INTRODUCING JOSEPH
AND HIS BROTHERS

The eleventh son of Jacob, we discover Joseph as a teenager in a very dysfunctional home. His father was a deceiver and a trickster. He was a manipulator by trade. One of the more infamous deceptions he is known for is tricking his father into giving him the birthright that was due to his older brother.

Jacob had twelve sons by four different women, which explain a lot of the dysfunction right there. In the midst of baby-mama-drama, the children grew up to create their own form of chaos. One of the sons, Reuben, had sex with one of his father's concubines. When Jacob found out about it—which he did—you could imagine what happened. Reality TV has nothing on Joseph's family. You may be able to keep up with the Kardashians in our world today, but I doubt anyone could keep up with Joseph and his brothers.

Two of Joseph's brothers, Simeon and Levi, were mass murderers. In Genesis 34:25 we read, "Now it came about on the third day, when they were in pain, that two of Jacob's sons, Simeon and Levi, Dinah's brothers, each took his sword and came upon the city unawares, and killed every male." Not surprisingly, these two brothers set up the township for murder through deception. They talked the entire town into getting circumcised and then brutally murdered them while they were healing and unable to fight back.

Then there was Joseph's brother Judah who had sexual relations with his daughter-in-law. Holidays in Joseph's home would have been, no doubt, a disaster. This was one messed up family. If we were looking for a home out of which to pick the future savior of an entire nation, and even the known world to a large degree, from starvation by famine, it is doubtful we would have landed on Jacob and his twelve sons. How could anything good come out of such mess?

Add on top of already volatile emotions the dynamics of favoritism and you have a concoction worthy of a witch's brew. In Genesis 37:3 we find just that, "Now Israel (Jacob) loved Joseph more than all his sons, because he was the son of his old age; and he made him a varicolored tunic." This is the verse where we are introduced to the famous "coat of many colors" which Jacob gave to his son, Joseph, sparking a fury of jealousy in the family.

Despite Joseph's messed up background and volatile history, God went on to use him in a position of great influence and respect. Describe how this makes you feel, and why it is important to recognize this aspect of Joseph's life.

What are some meanings that Joseph's "coat of many colors" might have given to his other family members and community members nearby?

Based on Genesis 37:3, why did Joseph's father love him more than the others? In what way did the fact that Joseph's mother was Rachel play into this favoritism?

Have you ever been the "favored one" or known someone who was the "favored one"? How does this reality impact other people's perceptions of and interactions with the so-called "favored one"?

Scripture pulls no punches in telling us how Joseph being the "favored one" made his brothers feel. We read, "His brothers saw that their father loved him more than all his brothers; and so they hated him and could not speak to him on friendly terms," (Gen. 37:4). Joseph's brothers hated him so much they couldn't even talk to him right.

Add to this storm the lightning and thunder of a dream and you have a recipe for murder. Shortly after getting the robe, Joseph had a dream in which he saw his brothers bowing down to him as sheaves of grain. At the tender age of seventeen, Joseph didn't have the wisdom to keep that type of dream to himself. So when he told his brothers about what he saw, they mocked him and said, "'Are you actually going to reign over us? Or are you really going to rule over us?' So they hated him even more for his dreams and for his words," (v. 8).

They already hated him just because of the coat of many colors. Pile the dream on top of that and they "hated him even more." Not only that, in verse 9 we discover Joseph had another dream. This time the sun, moon, and eleven stars bowed down to him. When he told his father about this dream, his father rebuked him for thinking that they would one day bow down to him. Joseph's dreams had even gone so far as to offend the one who loved him most. You can imagine what that did to his brothers.

Is it always wise to share your dreams and visions with others? Why or why not?

When might it be wise to keep your dreams to yourself or to a select few trusted friends or relatives?

What are some reactions you have seen or possibly given when someone shared a dream with you that seemed "unlikely" or "impossible"?

Wisdom is the ability to know when and what to share. Just because the Lord lays something on your heart doesn't mean you have to tell it to everyone. Joseph did not know this truth early on, and it cost him a lot. He wound up being left in a pit and later sold as a slave. Joseph still needed to be developed before the essence of his dream and vision could come true.

I know so many of us have dreams of shiny lives and magnificent futures—love like in the movies and careers that satisfy us while affording us our greatest desires. Yet God says, "I can't put you where you need to be until I clean you up first." He cannot give us our destiny if we will not allow Him to shape our character, to deal with our sins, flaws, fears, doubt, and immaturity. Until God is free to produce and promote righteousness within us, He is not free to move us to our intended destination. We have to take a detour first, second, third, and so on until we have been developed enough to handle what He has in store.

So few Christians understand that. If we could only grasp this truth and reality, it would make the way we view and go through trials entirely different. If we could see the purpose through the pain, we would bear up under it with a great deal more dignity. Because we don't, we often wind up like Joseph—learning lessons of loss, lust, and lies over and over and over ad nauseum.

When you look at where you are now emotionally, spiritually, and so on, what areas do you see where you still need to develop before being able to fully live out your destiny?

Read James 1:2-4. What is the purpose of detours (trials, testing)?

How does the purpose listed in James 1:2-4 differ from your viewpoint about trials, testing, or detours? In what ways does it align?

How can you help someone else who is going through a detour or trial understand this important truth without coming across as being "preachy" or "meddling"?

I can't imagine the pain God bears in witnessing our pain, especially when we can't understand what He is doing. When we blame Him, yell at Him, ignore Him, become bitter toward Him, and all along, He knows what He is allowing is for our good, His glory, and the benefit of those we love. He takes our punches and defends our blows because He knows that some day we will recognize His hand of kindness and direction, and thank Him.

You may be in a bad place right now. You may be in a pit like Joseph, without water, food, or fellowship. You may feel like you are the only one in a perfect storm designed specifically to take you down. But I want to speak to you in the middle of your detour. I want to ask you to make yourself available to God in whatever form or fashion He chooses. If you do, you will one day discover His divine providence in using the pain to strengthen your spirit and to deliver you from that pit or storm to that perfect place that is waiting for you.

God has a plan for you. Try not to fight the detours that are designed to take you to its culmination. Praise Him in the pain, even if it is just a faint word that falls off your parched lips. He knows what He is doing. He has great things up ahead for you.

Prayer

Dear Lord, I give You permission to develop me in order to prepare me for my destiny. I understand that this will require tests, trials, and detours along the way. I only ask that You make Yourself present to me in every way, reminding me along the way that You have a purpose to the pain and a greater good in mind. Make me into the person You most desire and allow me to serve You in ways I have previously only yet dreamed. In Christ's name, amen.

Day 4

THE LORD WAS WITH JOSEPH

When you fill a sponge full of water and then you squeeze the sponge, water is going to come out of it because it is full of water. When you are going through a trial and you feel the pressure of life caving in around you, how much of God comes out? Or is it cussing, fussing, complaining, and blaming that comes out instead? Why are those things coming out? Because that is what you are full of. A sponge only lets out what is in it.

Most people fill themselves with entertainment, alcohol, gossip, distractions, bitterness, and things of that nature when life is not fair. But in order to have your detour fulfill its purpose of taking you to your destiny, you have to draw near to God so that God will also be near to, and in, you.

The key to making it through your season of testing is not found in your contacts, notoriety, name, or bank account. The key is found in your intimacy with the Lord.

As we look more deeply at the life of Joseph, we discover that the Lord was with Joseph through the difficult times, even if it may not have appeared to be so at that time.

Read Genesis 37:21,22. In what way was God with Joseph when he was in the pit?

Read Genesis 37:26-28. How was God with Joseph in having him be sold to slave traders? In what way would this seemingly negative reality later prove to be a positive life detour?

Read Genesis 37:36. Why is it important to note that Joseph was sold to the "captain of the guard"? In what way does this indicate that God was with Joseph at this time as well?

When Joseph was in the pit, God sovereignly guided his every step, using the difficult detour to ultimately get Joseph in a position where he would one day rise to prominence. Not only that, but once Joseph arrived in Egypt, God was able to give Joseph favor in his position as a slave, and even later in prison. God was able to cause Joseph's hand to prosper and let other people give Joseph authority because God was with Joseph during the detours. What's more, Joseph was with God. We do not read of Joseph complaining, whining, or doubting what God had told him despite his dire situation.

Read Genesis 39:2-6.

> The Lord *was with Joseph, so he became a successful man. And he was in the house of his master, the Egyptian. Now his master saw that the* Lord *was with him and how the* Lord *caused all that he did to prosper in his hand. So Joseph found favor in his sight and became his personal servant; and he made him overseer over his house, and all that he owned he put in his charge. It came about that from the time he made him overseer in his house and over all that he owned, the* Lord *blessed the Egyptian's house on account of Joseph; thus the* Lord's *blessing was upon all that he owned, in the house and in the field. So he left everything he owned in Joseph's charge; and with him there he did not concern himself with anything except the food which he ate.*

Also read Genesis 39:21-23:

> But the Lord *was with Joseph and extended kindness to him, and gave him favor in the sight of the chief jailer. The chief jailer committed to Joseph's charge all the prisoners who were in the jail; so that whatever was done there, he was responsible for it. The chief jailer did not supervise anything under Joseph's charge because the* Lord *was with him; and whatever he did, the* Lord *made to prosper.*

Describe what you think it means when it says that the "LORD was with Joseph"?

Because the "LORD was with Joseph," what were some of the things the people in authority over Joseph gave to him?

Have you ever experienced favor in your life from someone in authority? Do you recognize God's hand in giving you this favor?

What did God give Joseph and do for him on his detour in Potiphar's house and in the prison?

In what ways has God prospered you while you have been on what seems to be a "detour" in your life?

Do you recognize a pattern of your trust in Him and His hand of favor and prosperity in your difficult situations?

Are there areas in your life right now where you need to trust God more? What practical steps can you take to do this?

One of the purposes of detours is to develop you to have the capacity, skills, and character you need to carry out your destiny. While Joseph was a slave in Potiphar's home, the Lord prospered him so that he became second in command in Potiphar's home. Little did he know that one day he would become second in command of the entire nation of Egypt. God was preparing Joseph with the skills necessary to both follow and lead simultaneously.

Joseph did not have the details of his destiny, but his obedience in his detours and his aim for excellence in all he did gave him the opportunity to learn skills he would use later on as a ruler.

Joseph acquired experience in leadership, management, handling staff, dealing with problems, and more. One of the problems we have today in our culture is that people want what they want right now. What we don't realize is that if you can't handle where you are now, how will you handle more responsibility later?

Read Jeremiah 12:5. How important is development of skills, character, mindsets and all else before being promoted to your destiny?

Who among your friends or family has gone through development when they felt they were on a detour but later came to discover how that played into their future destiny? Can you share about their experience and what encouragement it ought to give to yourself and others?

Look back at your last few years, or even a decade, and see if you can discern a pattern of God developing certain skills, character qualities, leadership abilities, and more in your life.

List three of these and share how God has used them to take you to your next level, or how you think He may want to in the future. Do any of them surprise you?

1.

2.

3.

Training for greater things always takes place in lesser things. Be faithful and responsible and content where you are now. That is one of the major secrets to God taking you further and giving you more.

God is not ready to give you your destiny until you can handle where you are now. How can you take care of your destiny there if you are not yet taking care of the destiny He has you in right here? You have to get enough experience first with the "this" you are in now before He gives you the "that" you are hoping for.

As a believer, you should be the best employee, the most on-time employee, the most productive employee because the Lord is with you. Translate that into any area—to be the best volunteer, spouse, parent, friend, etc. Your relationship with God should bring favor to those around you due to your integrity, honesty, morality—not theirs. You should stand out as Joseph stood out—wherever you are.

Prayer

Lord, I want You with me. I want You to show up in all that I do. Give me Your favor and develop a heart that seeks You first in everything. Help me live closely related to You, so much so that other people can't help but recognize it. Even in my detour, God, I want to glorify You. In Christ's name, amen.

Day 5

WHAT DETOURS ARE

Let's take a moment to review what we've covered this week. First, we looked at what detours are. We also looked at how they may feel like a negative thing we don't want, but if we look at them through the lens of God's purpose, we can discover they are good after all.

Next, we talked about the importance of development on the path to our destiny. We looked at a few biblical people who experienced significant detours such as Moses, Abraham, and Paul. Then we went deeper into the life of Joseph on Day Three. Since Joseph serves as the basis for our study on detours, we started his story at the beginning where we found him in a very dysfunctional family.

Yesterday, we introduced the concept of sovereignty—a concept we will look at in greater detail later on. We examined how even in those times that it didn't appear that God was with Joseph that He was, in fact, working things out to accomplish His intended purpose. And later, as Joseph inched closer to his destiny, we saw how God brought favor, authority, and prosperity to Joseph in the midst of his being in positions of servitude and slavery.

Today, as we conclude our time looking at the purpose of our detours, I want to add a few more important things. One of them is something we touched on briefly before—that is God using Joseph's detour to literally take him someplace he didn't plan to go.

Sometimes detours God will use detours to re-route us to an entirely new location that we wouldn't have even thought of going to ourselves. Yes, it would be nice if God simply spoke to us like He did Abraham and tell us to go to a land unknown. It would also be nice if we would have the courage to respond as Abraham did. But far too often we either fail to hear, or if we do hear, we fail to follow because it just doesn't make sense. So God ties us up, as He did Joseph behind some camels, and He finds a way to get us there anyhow.

The problem comes if you or I only see the camels. The frustration happens if you or I only see the ropes. If we only feel the hot sun or the hunger and emptiness night after night and miss seeing what God is doing—we will miss the divine purpose of the detour.

God allows people to move us, shape us, and take us to our next step on the path He wants us to travel. So never think that just because it's people you see that it isn't God directing behind the scenes. God will often use people—even people in your family, even messed up people in your family—to move you to your destiny through a detour.

Read 2 Kings 6:15-18. In what way was God working behind the scenes to bring about His ultimate good in this situation?

Name or describe a time in your life, or someone's you know, where God was arranging things behind the scenes to usher in the next scenario.

Read 2 Kings 8:1-6. Describe the critical nature of "timing" in how God brought about a positive solution to this woman's dilemma. Why is it important to wait on God's perfect timing?

Timing matters—which is how it always is with God. It's a matter of timing. It's a matter of Him setting up the intersections of life so that when you get there, the people you are connecting with are ready for you. And, even more importantly, you are ready to handle what has been given to you as well.

Is there something you are waiting on that God has put in your heart? Describe how you feel about the wait and how a perspective on God's perfect timing helps you to wait with expectation.

Read Ecclesiastes 3:1. What does this verse tell you about life's ebbs and flows and the purpose of our detours?

It's easy to worship God and surrender to Him when all is well and life doesn't seem to have any detours, isn't it? It's not easy when you are in a jail, like Joseph wound up in. But for us, jails come in all shapes and sizes. It may be an emotional jail. A relational jail—like a relationship you wish you were never in but have no way out of, or a relationship you wish you had but are, at the moment, alone. Your jail could one of finances or health or even your job.

Are you in a holding pattern emotionally, relationally, career-wise, or in any other way? In what way does this impact your worship of God?

Take some time to identify ways you can improve your relationship with God in the midst of your detours and disappointments.

Prayer

Lord Jesus, I am choosing to humble myself before You as I discover Your purposes for detours in my life. Help me to open my mind and my heart to learn about Your ways and reasons for allowing things in me and to me. Use this Bible study as a time to develop me spiritually so that I become more and more like Your Son, Jesus Christ, in my attitudes and in my character. In Christ's name, amen.

Week 2

THE PROOF OF
DETOURS

Start

Welcome everyone to session 2 of Detours.

What was a helpful point of review or a new insight gained from your personal study last week?

Does anybody have any stories or updates related to our discussion and application from the previous group session?

As we continue to study Joseph's story, and the detours God took him on, notice how God uses detours in our own lives to bring us closer to Him. Sometimes detours take longer than we hoped for, but remember that the Lord has a purpose and a reason for them and that we can trust His timing.

Have you recognized detours in your life that you didn't realize were detours at the time?

Before we see what Dr. Evans has to continue teach us about detours, would somebody pray for our time together? Especially ask the Lord to open our hearts and minds to His Word?

Watch

Complete this viewer guide as you watch the video for session 2.

You know you are on a detour when:

1. God allows the same thing to happen to you _twice_.

      God confirms the truth and application of His Word through _repetition_ of the same _sermon_.

2. You're suffering for being _righteous_.

3. God gives you glimpses of His _presence_ even while your _situation_ has not changed.

4. God gives you people to _serve_ who are in the same _situation_ you are.

      Ministry during times of _misery_ is critical.

5. God _____ your _____ when you think you had one.

6. Sometimes you have to take by _faith_ what you do not _feel_.

7. God delays until your _development_ and your _destiny_ connect.

Respond

Discuss the video with your group, using the questions below.

Have you ever been on a detour that led to another detour? Maybe an alternate route that had a repair or accident on it that required yet another change of route? Explain.

Namer a time when you have realized that you were on a God-ordained detour?

Have there been "two-witness" scenarios in your life, where God has repeated a situation to get your attention? Share your experience with the group.

Have you ever done something that was the righteous thing to do in the sight of God but you suffered as a result of it? What lessons did you learn from that experience?

Read 2 Timothy 3:12. When have you been persecuted for livingf or God?

Read 1 Peter 2:20. What does God promise us in our suffering?

How has God given you glimpses or even full-on assurance of His presence when you have suffered?

How has God used an unlikely person in your life to guide you to the next stage of your detour?

What does Dr. Evans mean when he said, "Sometimes you have to take by faith what you do not feel."? How have you experienced this statement in your own life?

How have you mistakenly credited luck or fate in a situation where you now recognize it as God's providence?

Read week 2 and complete the activities before the next group session.

Under Construction

Part of my role as pastor involves mentoring and counseling. With a fairly large church, you can imagine the number of calls I get. I can honestly say I enjoy this aspect of being a pastor immensely. Not too long ago, one of the men from the church came over to my home to meet with me. He had been going through a rough time.

As he sat in my family room, head hung low, he lifted his eyes to mine and said, "Pastor, I feel as if my detour has met another detour and they got married and had a baby detour." In other words, he felt as he were running into detour after detour after detour and that the detours merely kept replicating and multiplying rather than taking him anywhere meaningful.

It is easy to feel that way when God is taking you to your destiny. This is because before you can ever get to where God wants you to be, He has to do some twists and turns. In life, as it is often on the road, detours exist because construction is taking place. When you are on a highway and there is a detour, it is usually because workers are trying to fix, build, correct, or improve something.

Similarly, God will take us on a detour because He is constructing something in our lives as well. Granted, detours are anything but convenient. They take you out of the way. They are longer than you originally had planned to travel. But they are necessary. God is more interested in your development than your arrival. He cares more for your character than your comfort, more for your purity than your productivity.

In this week's lesson, I want us to look at ways to help us determine and confirm that we truly are on a detour, rather than simply experiencing a bad circumstance. How can we know that this is a God-ordained detour rather than things just aren't working out right now?

How can you discern that you are not under the circumstances of normal life and consequences but rather in a situation that God Himself has guided you into? We will answer those questions, and more, up ahead. Keep driving.

Day 1
SUFFERING FOR DOING RIGHT

After Joseph had worked in his master Potiphar's home for some time, he had earned Potiphar's trust. So much so, that Joseph was over pretty much everything in Potiphar's home.

Potiphar's wife had noticed that Joseph was attractive, so she made advances at him—day after day (Gen.39:6-10). However, Joseph was wise enough to pass on the passes. He was wise enough from God's perspective, that is.

From man's perspective, that decision to refuse the request of his master's wife landed him on the hot seat and ultimately in another pit as she, in her pain of rejection, accused him of rape.

Read Genesis 39:19-20. Does this verse tell us if Joseph had the opportunity to tell his side of the story?

What happened to Joseph as a result of this accusation?

How do you think Joseph felt knowing he had made a moral decision but seemingly wound up worse off because of it?

Have you ever done something that was "right" in the sight of God, but suffered as a result of it? What lessons did you learn from this experience?

When you find yourself, like Joseph, struggling or suffering as the result of a decision you made in obedience to God, your struggle is right where God wants you to be. This is actually one "proof" that you are on a detour:

If and when you are suffering for doing good rather than doing bad, we also call that being persecuted for righteousness, you can know you are in a God-planned detour.

If we look more closely at the biblical account of Joseph and Potiphar's wife, it clearly tells us that Joseph refused her out of obedience to the Lord. He said, "Behold, with me here, my master does not concern himself with anything in the house, and he has put all that he owns in my charge. There is no one greater in this house than I, and he has withheld nothing from me except you, because you are his wife. How then could I do this great evil and sin against God?" (Gen. 39:8-9).

Joseph recognized the blessings in his life and felt gratitude for how far God had taken him—from a pit left to die to a position of great authority and responsibility in a foreign land. Knowing his source was God Himself, Joseph made his decision on God alone.

Reflect on a time or situation when you were tempted to sin but instead chose not to out of your love and gratitude toward God.

How did God respond to you at that time or even later in life as a result of your decision to resist temptation?

Read 2 Timothy 3:12 and summarize it in your own words.

This part of Joseph's story is not one we normally discuss, but I think it is important. We are never told this exactly, but it could be that Potiphar's wife was an actual temptation to Joseph. It could be that she was attractive, the servants were away, Potiphar, also, was gone, and Joseph may have felt something for her. We don't know.

What I do know is that a sacrifice isn't a sacrifice unless it costs you something (1 Chron. 21:24; 2 Sam. 24:24). And a temptation isn't a temptation unless it's tempting. Knowing this, it underscores the reality that Joseph turned her offer down out of his conviction before God, not necessarily out of a lack of interest. That's important to keep in mind as you go through life and make decisions.

As God did in testing Abraham by asking him to offer up the child of his heart as a sacrifice (Gen. 22), God will also often ask us to sacrifice or overcome a temptation out of our love and obedience for Him, something that costs us something as well. This decision cost Joseph the loss of potential pleasure, his job, and ultimately his freedom.

List three examples of temptations for you. You can keep them vague such as overeating, a relationship, etc.

1.

2.

3.

List three approaches you can take to overcome these temptations out of your love for and commitment to God. Will you spend some time in prayer asking God to help you to do so?

1.

2.

3.

If you are a serious believer and you are making decisions based on what God wants over what you or even your friends or society in general want, the Bible says you can be sure that there will be persecution. There will be suffering. There will be sacrifice. It may come in different shapes, sizes, and forms—but it will come. Negative repercussions follow those who live by faith.

In fact, if you never get negative repercussions in your life for godly decisions you make then that is a good sign that you are not living solidly as a Christian. The Bible says clearly that those who make their choices based on their faith (who desire to live godly) will be persecuted. Everyone is not going to be your friend if you are serious about Jesus. This is because you will have to make choices that go against the grain.

Scripture gives us the following verses about suffering for God:

- Acts 5:41: "So they went on their way from the presence of the Council, rejoicing that they had been considered worthy to suffer shame for His name."
- Acts 9:16: "I will show him how much he must suffer for My name's sake."
- 1 Peter 2:20: "For what credit is there if, when you sin and are harshly treated, you endure it with patience? But if when you do what is right and suffer for it you patiently endure it, this finds favor with God."
- Romans 8:17: " ...and if children, heirs also, heirs of God and fellow heirs with Christ, if indeed we suffer with Him so that we may also be glorified with Him."
- Philippians 3:10: "My goal is to know Him and the power of His resurrection and the fellowship of His sufferings, being conformed to His death," (HCSB).

Read 2 Timothy 2:12 and write it in your own words:

Read Hebrews 11:25 and write it in your own words:

Based on all of these verses, what do we learn about the nature, condition, and biblical perspective of suffering for righteousness?

Daniel was thrown into the lion's den because he wouldn't compromise on the job. Meshach, Shadrach, and Abednego got tossed into a fiery furnace for refusing to bow to an idol. They suffered the effects of their decision to not compromise their faith. It is unfortunate today how few Christians are willing to bear consequences for their commitment. Too many believers today are moving along as cultural Christians, or convenient Christians—not so many are committed Christians.

The most critical test you will ever face is the test for suffering when you did nothing wrong. When you do exactly what God has told you to do and you have to pay a price tag for it, you are paying a penalty for righteousness sake. You are on an intended detour that will test and strengthen both your character and your resolve if you will let it.

The greater the calling, the deeper the pit. The higher the destiny, the tighter the shackles. The more glorious the future, the more persecuted the present. Learn to view suffering (when suffering for good) through the lens of the Lord. He has a purpose for the pain if you will discover how to hang in there—like Joseph—even when life does not seem fair.

Prayer

Loving heavenly Father, give me the heart, patience, and perspective to view my suffering for righteousness' sake as a blessing rather than a curse. I want my detour to accomplish its intended aim, God, so help me to get in alignment under You with my thoughts, heart, and actions in order to honor You in the face of unjust or undeserved suffering.

Day 2
YOU ARE NOT ALONE

Do you remember in school when the teacher would grade on the curve? At first when this decision was announced, it would give everyone hope. It would make us believe that we had a chance at a great grade because if the subject matter was difficult, our doing poorly may be good enough after all. But then, if your class was anything like mine, there would always be that one person, or two, who would somehow manage to ace the test even though the rest of us got low Bs or even Cs. Those amazing scores would cause the curve to not mean much or anything at all. We called that breaking the curve where I came from.

When you are chosen by God to represent Him in the culture, He wants you to break the curve. He wants you to set the standard so high that you truly reflect Him in your life. When you choose righteousness, and suffer because of it, the Lord will often allow continual trials because He knows they will test you even further. They will produce in you the qualities and character that will make you more like Jesus Christ. Joseph had a glorious destiny ahead of him. He had a destiny that would save people—save nations—from literal starvation. But Joseph wasn't going to arrive at his destiny until his character was molded and shaped in a manner where he could handle his destiny well.

Have you experienced this in your own life or in the life of someone you know, where God has asked you to set a standard that is higher than those around you? Or when it has seemed that God has continually allowed you to be in trial after trial due to no known fault of your own? Describe your mindset to these situations and what gave you the courage to stay strong.

In yesterday's lesson we looked at one way to discover if you are on a God-inspired detour or simply going through the consequences of bad choices. We saw how suffering for what is right is often a way that God tests us. Joseph wound up in jail because he refused to dishonor God by accepting the advances of Potiphar's wife.

Another way you can discern you are on a detour designed by God is that in the midst of your suffering for doing good, God shows you His presence. He shows you His favor. God joins you in the pit.

Read Daniel 3:24-26. How many men were originally tossed into the fire?

How many people did the king see when he looked into the fire?

God's presence with the three men in the fire not only freed them from the restraints that bound their arms, but it also protected them from what should have killed them. In addition to that, because of what the king witnessed when seeing them walk around, he told his guards to release the men. Thus, God's presence delivered the men out of the fire as well. God's presence is powerful. It brings comfort, protection, and deliverance in the most trying of times.

Describe a time in your life, or in the life of someone you know, where God's presence brought about a noticeable change in a difficult situation.

How can we as individuals provide the opportunity for God to join us more often? What did the three men and Joseph all do that led to God being with them?

Is there something in your life that you need to yield in obedience to God right now? Take a moment to pray about this or to ask God to reveal this to you. You can also thank God in advance for His powerful presence which will be with you in times of difficulties that arise from obeying Him.

Before we go any further, stop and examine your own views on obedience to God.

Read John 14:15 and Luke 6:46. What are your initial reactions to these verses from the Gospels?

Based on these verses, are we to be obedient based on extrinsic motivation (external reward or consequence) or intrinsic motivation (internal desire)?

How does this reality shift our mindset to one of acceptance when things externally may go wrong (according to the human viewpoint) even after we have obeyed?

There is a lot of confusion today between the connection of obedience to blessing. Many believers assume that if they are obedient to God, they ought to deserve a tangible reward. We live in a rewards-based culture and that mentality has drifted into the Christian worldview in many ways. However, based on Scripture, many people were worse off in the tangible world when they obeyed. After all, Jesus' obedience led Him to a cross. It is only when we align our understanding of obedience with God's overarching sovereign hand of purpose (and even pruning) that we will be able to approach and go through our detours with faith, trust, and dignity rather than doubt.

Far more often than not, the proof that you are on a divinely-designed detour will come from the realization of God's presence in the midst of difficulty. It will not come from the immediate removal of difficulty (although that can occur) but rather from the persevering and preserving power given to you by God Himself as you go through the detour.

God didn't keep Daniel from the lion's den; He met him in it. He didn't keep Shadrach, Meshach, and Abednego from the fiery furnace; He joined them in it. He didn't keep Joseph from being a slave to Potiphar; He gave him favor in it. And

He met him in the prison as well. The second proof in knowing you are where God wants you to be in your detour is that God doesn't deliver you from it but rather joins you in it.

Prayer

Loving Christ, teach me how to recognize Your presence in the midst of my trials and detours. Help me to focus more on You than on my detour. Forgive my complaints, doubt, and desire to exit quickly from what You have designed not only for my development but also as a future testimony to Your goodness and grace. I adore You and ask that You will reveal Yourself to me all the more through times of testing. In Christ's name, amen.

Day 3

TWICE IS A CHARM

If you'll remember when Joseph was a slave in Potiphar's house, Potiphar promoted him and made him head over everything. Later, when Joseph languished in jail, the same thing happened. The jailer took notice of him and put him in charge over everything at the prison. God showed up twice in a very similar way.

Scripture often says that by two or three witnesses a matter will be confirmed (2 Cor. 13:1; Deut. 19:15). When the Lord shows up twice in your life in a similar fashion, pay attention. He is talking. It's not bad luck. It's not good luck. It's not chance. It is God confirming He is doing this on purpose because He is giving you a double witness.

When Gideon needed proof that he was really hearing from God, he put the animal skin out and asked for God to make it dry on one side and wet on the other. The next day he flipped it over and asked for the opposite. God will often reveal Himself in groups of two. Not always, but there is often a pattern you can see if you look through spiritual eyes.

Read 2 Corinthians 13:1. Why is it important to confirm things through two or three witnesses?

Now read Isaiah 55:11. God speaks to you through His Word. Describe a time God confirmed something in your life through two or three Scriptures that stood out to you.

Based on Acts 5:32, do the two or three witnesses have to only come from people? Who else and what else can be a witness of God's confirming message or guidance in your life?

Look for how God might be speaking to you by doing or allowing something twice in your life. Ask Him for wisdom to discern His hand of favor and what it means. Sometimes it may mean no real change in your situation—you may still be in the pit—but just knowing you are not alone is enough to give you the strength to wait.

> **Read Genesis 40:1-8. Briefly describe what had happened and how Joseph responded. Note the occurrence of twice. What two ways does "twice" show up in this passage (reflect back on Joseph's ability to interpret his own dream as a young man for one of the instances)?**

> **1.**

> **2.**

> **Is God, or has God, confirmed any situation in your life through this pattern of "twice"? Share some of the details and what you learned from the experience.**

When you want to know if it's just chance, or Satan trying to trick you, or even just your own wishful thinking, look for the pattern of repetition. Look for twice. God will always confirm His will. He will always validate His Word. Interestingly, two years after the cupbearer and the baker were released from jail, Pharaoh had a dream (Gen. 41:1).

> **Read Genesis 41:32. Notice Joseph's reference to God's pattern of "twice." What conclusion does Joseph draw about God's use of "twice"?**

> **Why do you think Joseph stated the matter would be carried out soon since the dream was given twice?**

In what way can you apply the realization of this pattern of proof that God uses to your own life?

Recognizing patterns in our lives sometimes gets lost in the everyday busyness that consumes a lot of our time and attention. Be mindful to pay attention to what God is doing in your life, and in particular the repetition of similar things God does or says to you. If you are on a detour, this reality can bring you comfort knowing that you are not alone and trusting that God has a purpose for where you are right now.

Prayer

Lord and Savior, open my eyes to see ways that
You communicate to me. Help me not to miss the
spiritual connections You make through things that
happen or things I read in Your Word. I want to
know Your will and Your way so give me wisdom and
insight to do that well. In Christ's name, amen.

Day 4
SURPRISE!

In yesterday's lesson, we looked at one clue that can let you know when you are in a God-ordained detour, as opposed to just running into a difficult time—when God shows up in a similar fashion or communicates a similar message twice. Like Gideon and his fleece set out twice to confirm his answer, God will often repeat a matter in order to affirm the mindset He wants you to have toward your detour.

In today's lesson, I want us to look at another proof you are in a God-ordained detour and that this is when God may surprise you.

Has God ever come out of nowhere in a situation in your life to turn it around or provide for you? Describe what happened and what you learned from it.

Read Genesis 22:13. What is the surprise in this passage?

Was there any way for Abraham to predict how God would provide a sacrifice? Is it common to find rams on a hillside caught in a bush?

Apply what you learned from Genesis 22:13 to a situation you may be facing right now or have faced in the past. In what way do you need to release to God the "how" of what you need provided or changed? Take a moment to pray and let Him know you are trusting Him even though the "how" may be a mystery right now.

For two full years, Joseph sat in jail having hoped that the cupbearer would remember him. I'm sure after some time, he assumed the cupbearer would not. He probably felt forgotten, overlooked, and even skipped by God. Waiting for that knock on the door that never came, I wonder if Joseph even bothered to keep track of the days.

After that long, would you? After that long, have you?

Are you somewhere in your life where you feel forgotten, overlooked or even skipped by God? Have you been praying for, waiting for, and hoping for His hand of intervention to no avail? Do you feel trapped, stuck, or as if you are in a hopeless situation? If that's you, then not only is today's lesson for you but so is this entire study. Hang in there—God has something to speak to your heart about where you are right now. One of the primary principles is that after preparation and development have run their course, God is ready to do to you and through you what He planned all along. How that comes about will often surprise you.

Let's look at how God did it with Joseph. While Joseph sat yet another day in jail, the wisdom of the wisest men in Egypt fell short for Pharaoh who had experienced alarming and confusing dreams. This left Pharaoh at a loss for what to do next. That is, until the cupbearer spoke up.

Read Genesis 41:9, "Then the chief cupbearer said to Pharaoh, "Today I remember my faults" (HCSB). Notice the word *remember*. What did God cause the cupbearer to remember?

How many years had it been since the cupbearer last interacted with Joseph? (Refer to Genesis 41:1).

Is there something in your life that you thought was going to be brought about, changed, fixed, or redeemed but several years have passed since you first had that belief? How does this passage encourage you to just hang in there and wait well for God's timing?

Read Genesis 41:10-14. Summarize the words of the cupbearer and tell what happened as a result of his testimony to Pharaoh?

Some people may call what happened in that meeting between Pharaoh and the cupbearer luck, chance, or happenstance. Some may even call it fate. But as a believer in God, none of those words should even be in your vocabulary. What happened that day is providence. Providence is the hand of God moving in the glove of history—giving a dream, having set up the dream-reader, and reminding the cupbearer about his connection from years before.

In volleyball, one player will often set a ball. Setting is one of the fundamental types of hitting in the game. It is a strategic move that sets up another player to come and spike the ball, driving it down like a missile, into the opponent's side of the net. Once a ball is set, the other player runs up to it and hits it forcefully in an area that will be difficult to defend for the other side. In volleyball, it always takes two players to set and then spike a ball. But, as we see so often in Scripture and as this powerful illustration of Joseph's life reminds us, God Himself is constantly setting things up ahead of time and then spiking them for a point in our lives.

It was God who set the situation up for the cupbearer so he could remember Joseph from prison. In order for that to happen, God orchestrated two dreams two years earlier while the cupbearer and the baker were in jail. Then, He sovereignly arranged for Joseph to correctly interpret those dreams. Next, He providentially fulfilled the interpretation of those dreams. Finally, two years later, He gave Pharaoh two dreams which could not be interpreted by Pharaoh's key advisors. Thus, the spike. The cupbearer remembered that "Hebrew man" in jail and recommended him to his agitated and frustrated leader.

Take some time to look back over your life and to identify patterns where God has prepared beforehand something He carried out later in your life. Share how you felt before you saw it all "come together" and how you felt after.

Are you willing to see your faith increased in times of waiting, trusting that God is providentially setting things up for His perfect moment to act? What steps can you take to actively live out this increased level of faith?

We read in Genesis 41:8 that after Pharaoh sent for Joseph, Joseph shaved and changed his clothes. Having sat in the horrid environment of a dungeon for so long, it was time for a makeover. But that's exactly what God will do. When He brings you out of your detour and into your destiny, He cleans you up. He gets you ready. He transforms not only your soul but all there is to you. God can take off those jail clothes when He removes you from a negative reality, giving you a fresh start and a fresh face.

If you ever want to do a study in the Bible, I recommend doing one on the word *suddenly*. Suddenly is when God surprises you, when He comes out of nowhere, when you couldn't have planned it or created it yourself.

Suddenly.

You think you are stuck somewhere but then suddenly, God shows you you've already arrived.

Prayer

Dear Lord, I choose to trust in You even in the times
when I do not see how You will bring about a change
or provide what I need. Your ways are higher than my
ways and Your thoughts are beyond my comprehension.
Remind me to let go of anxious attempts at trying to figure
out what You will do and to instead rest in the assurance
of Your providential hand. In Christ's name, amen.

Day 5

GOD CAN WORK IT OUT

When I was a boy growing up in Baltimore, my daddy bought me a balloon punching bag. I loved that balloon punching bag. No matter what I did to it, it kept bouncing back. I'd hit it—boom! It'd hit the floor. But then—bam! It'd bounce back up. I'd hit it again—boom! But then—bam! It'd be right back up. Over and over and over I'd hit this bag and it would bounce up for more.

The reason that balloon punching bag kept coming back for more was that there was a weight in the bottom that was heavier than the air in the bag at the top. No matter what I did to it up top, down below determined where things wound up.

That illustration leads us to another proof that you are on a God-ordained detour. You will have proof that God is working on your behalf because every time it looks like you are going down, you bounce back. Every time it looks like that should be the last straw, or you could never make it through, somehow you manage to regain your footing and get back up. You stand your ground.

Have you ever seen someone who manages to come through trial after trial, discouragement after discouragement? Take note of that person if you do. That is a person's whose faith is deeply weighted with the living God. That is a person who understands and believes that no matter what may happen, all things are definitely working out for good.

In what ways do you notice God working things out for good in your life?

Lastly, a proof that your detours are part of God's ordained plan for your life is when you see God help you in ways that you cannot explain. God has ways that are based on nothing tangible at all, and when He uses them, only He gets the credit. When Joseph was moved from the prison to the palace, He had no other way to explain it except for God.

Read Genesis 41:14-16. Compare and contrast Joseph's spirit in his response to Pharaoh here with the spirit he had toward his brothers as a teenager. In what way had Joseph matured?

Is there something in your life that has happened which can only be explained that it was done by God?

Joseph wound up second-in-command in Egypt off of a coat he never even asked to have—and some downtime in jail interpreting dreams. Not only that, he wound up with the authority and ability to move his whole family to Egypt and enable them to have plenty to eat during a time of worldwide famine. God used one mess after another mess and one situation after another situation to bring him to his destiny. Success is not in what you have. Success is in Who you have.

What role does obedience play in God moving us into a new season and position?

God doesn't need more than a minute to completely change your life and usher you into your destiny. What's more, He will more often than not do it in a way you could have never anticipated or even prepared for. When He does, He gets the credit for what He has done. This allows us to remain humble, knowing that it was God's hand who moved us into the place He wants us to be.

If you recognize any of these proofs that you are on a God-ordained detour currently, then wait on Him to move. Let go of the need to figure out "how" God will move, and simply trust instead that He will.

Prayer

Loving Lord and Savior, You can make a way where there seems to be no way. You are the ultimate One in control. Forgive me for trying to maneuver my life to my own destination rather than trusting that You are wiser, more powerful, and more gracious than I could ever even know. I yield my life to you and my detour, thanking You in advance for the upcoming destination. In Christ's name, amen.

Week 3

THE PATIENCE OF *DETOURS*

Start

Welcome everyone to session 3 of Detours.

What was a helpful point of review or a new insight gained from your personal study last week?

What stories or updates related to our discussion does anyone have? How were you able to apply what you learned from the previous group session?

In this session we'll turn our attention to the patience required when we find ourselves taking detours.

Have you ever been in a situation that seemed it would never end? From a lingering red light to a long wait in the doctors office, some situations seem to take longer than they should. Share with the group a time when you've experienced the frustration of waiting.

As Dr. Evans explained, there's no way to have a detour without extending the journey, and detours are critical for development. Sometimes we have to wait, even in our pain, as God develops us for the next stage of our destiny. Today, Dr. Evans will explore the patience that these detours require and what we should do while we wait.

Before we see what Dr. Evans has to teach us about patience, would somebody pray for our time together, asking the Lord to open our hearts and minds to what we can learn from His Word today?

Detours

Watch

Complete this viewer guide as you watch the video for session 3.

There is a time that God's Word to you is going to come to pass when the __test__ __is__ __over__.

Waiting on God means __not__ __going__ __outside__ of God to __resolve__ the issue.

The __temptation__ in waiting is __disobedience__.

Waiting on God means __worshiping__ while you wait.

Waiting on God means to __hold__ __on__ __to__ Him.

God __knows__ what He's doing, even when you think He's __doing__ __nothing__.

God allows __scenarios__ to take us __further__ than we would be without it.

The longer we do not __grow__ in the patience of __biblical__ __waiting__, the longer it's going to take for God to take us right where He wants us to be.

Respond

Discuss the video with your group, using the questions below.

Have you ever felt like God has you idling while you're in a detour? Explain.

How have you ever questioned your faith while you're waiting in a life detour?

Share examples of people in the Bible who had to wait on God. How do they and their examples encourage you?

How have you experienced the pain of forced patience?

While you've waited, have you ever tried to go outside of God to resolve the issue? What happened? What did you learn?

What are some of the lessons you've learned about God when you've waited?

Read John 21:20-23. Like Peter, how have you compared your season of waiting with someone else's? How has this affected your attitude in waiting?

What does Dr. Evans mean: "The longer we do not grow in the patience of biblical waiting, the longer it's going to take for God to take us where He wants us to be."?

Describe how you've seen patience modeled for you.

How have you practiced patience in the past? How will you begin to intentionally practice patience in your life?

Read week 3 and complete the activities before the next group session.

Patience and Purpose

Several years ago I had gone with my wife to Hawaii for a speaking engagement. Since we don't get over to Hawaii very often, we decided to add on a few additional days for rest and relaxation. The plans had been made. The weather was perfect. I finished my speaking engagement and we were both ready to relax.

The first few days went by fine but then something happened that I will never forget. Before I could even know what hit me, I was suddenly ravaged by a pain level I had never felt before. Now, I'm a man, and if you know me at all, you know that I pride myself on being a "kingdom man." However, in this moment in time, even a kingdom man had to yell out in agony. I suddenly had a lot of compassion for any woman who has ever given birth. The pain was so unbearable that I could barely speak and I felt like I was about to pass out.

Lois quickly arranged for transportation, and we headed to the nearest hospital. Now, don't get me wrong, I'm grateful for hospitals. I'm thankful for doctors. And I appreciate the fact that they have to gather all of the proper information before they can begin administering treatment. I don't want them to make a mistake, so I understand that processes are important. However, when you are seized by unspeakable pain, filling out forms or waiting in a chair for them to call your name is the last thing you want to do. Minutes felt like a millennium. If you have ever been in an emergency room, then you know exactly what I mean.

Waiting is no fun when you are in pain. In fact, waiting is no fun anytime. Really. We get impatient in lines that are too long at the store. We sigh in traffic that impedes our forward progress at the speed we want to go. We want our food as soon as we place the order. Our nation is certainly the home of the free and the land of the brave, but it isn't exactly a melting pot of patience.

Bu patience is a virtue we all need. So when God puts you or me on a detour that seems to be taking too long—and especially when the wait includes pain— patience, when practiced rightly, can quite possibly even speed up the path to your purpose. This week we are going to look at patience.

Day 1
WAITING WELL

Have you ever been at a red light that won't seem to ever go green? You feel stuck. Trapped. Held back from where you want to go. The circumstance in front of you simply won't let you move forward. Or, how about being stuck behind a slow moving vehicle on a narrow road that won't provide room to pass?

How about this? Have you ever been on the phone and the person on the other end of the line asks you to hold and then plays music? We all have at some point or another. It may only be minutes, but it can feel like hours as you sit and listen to music that really should never be called music at all.

All of those kinds of waiting are inconvenient. All of them test and try our patience. They can strip the smile straight off our faces. But, really the worst kind of waiting comes when you or I have to wait on God, when God forces you to wait for things to get better in your life, for things to improve, for your change to come.

It is in these times when it feels as if nothing is happening and God has put your life in neutral—your motor is running but the wheels aren't turning—that can cause the most pain.

List three times God has made you wait—or is asking you to wait right now—for something longer than you anticipated.

1.

2.

3.

Read Psalm 27:14 and Psalm 33:20-22. What are some components and mindsets for waiting well?

What is a positive outcome that waiting produces in us?

Sometimes it seems that God takes so long that you begin to wonder if believing in Him is the wisest thing to do. You begin to wonder if it's even worth the effort. You talk to God. You pray to Him. You made a prayer closet. It did no good. You go to church. You still feel empty and stuck. You worship, but nothing has changed. After a while you begin to feel that the relationship is too one-sided. Then, when things only get worse, you may even consider pulling back, withholding worship, prayer, or devotion because it just doesn't make much sense anymore. The clock keeps ticking. The years keep changing. The calendar keeps moving. God keeps delaying His response.

Read Hebrews 11:6. What do you learn from this verse regarding the opportunity that waiting on God provides?

Have you ever pulled back on worship, prayer, or time with God because a delay in an answer or change seemed to take too long? What does/did that action of withdrawing from the closeness in your relationship with God indicate?

Based on Hebrews 11:6, is that indication (from the previous question) pleasing to God? Why or why not?

Holding patterns in life are just as frustrating, if not more so, as holding patterns on flights. I fly a lot. Weekly, in fact. So I have become all too familiar with holding patterns. They can be even more difficult to wait through then the flight itself because on the flight you have an idea of how much longer you have to wait, but in a holding pattern, the answer to that question is left up in the air (pun intended!).

You just circle and circle and circle and circle, only to circle some more. And as you circle in the air or in life on your detour, the same result often occurs. Your soul loses the hope to even hope for something different.

Yet over and over again in the Bible we are told to "wait on the Lord." It is not something that appears once or twice. The phrase and concept to "wait on the Lord" is a frequent occurrence.

Read the following verses and write down similarities that show up between them.

Psalm 130:5-6   Psalm 27:13-14   Lamentations 3:25-26a

Similarities in approach and/or outcomes:

1.

2.

3.

4.

5.

Waiting is rarely easy. Whether it's for a movie to start at the theater, the day to end at work, a meal to be served in a restaurant, or something much more significant, waiting often tries our patience time and time again. But what we will discover through this look at the life of Joseph is that some things are worth the wait. Oftentimes, the greater the destiny, the longer the wait. God is doing things during the waiting period to prepare all the parts and pieces so they work in sync.

God has perfect timing. God's timing is never early, and it's never late. Because of that, waiting on God requires patience and an extra heaping of faith.

Prayer

Loving Lord, grow in me the ability to wait well. Help me to increase the level of patience I exhibit in the normal, daily activities of life. I want to please you with a patient spirit so increase my faith to trust that You are orchestrating things to come about in the perfect time and in the perfect way. In Christ's name, amen.

Day 2
WHEN GOD TARRIES

Do you fish? I can't say I fish often, but I have fished when the kids were younger. My daughter Priscilla has become quite the fisherwoman as there is a pond nearby their house that she and her husband can walk to with their sons. I admire Priscilla, but I can't say I'm jealous of her pond access and fishing skills. This is because I've never seemed to master this thing called fishing.

No matter how hard I try, it usually seems like I wind up fishing in ponds where nothing bites. Maybe you know what I'm talking about. You can stand there or sit there for hours, tossing line after line into the water, hooking worm after worm onto the line. Ultimately, it may feel like you are no longer fishing—you are just cruelly drowning worms. Ever been there? Someone walks by and asks what you are doing and you politely answer, "Just drowning some worms."

Waiting for your destiny—for your change, for your release from a detour to happen—can feel like drowning sometimes too. Except in this case, it is not the worms that are drowning. Instead, your dreams are drowning. Your desires are drowning. Your thoughts are drowning. Your opportunity is drowning. Your motivation is drowning. Your get-up-and-go is drowning. Nothing seems to be hooking onto the hope you toss out time and time again.

Truth be told, in your private moments—those moments alone that only you and God share—you may even feel like bailing on God, pulling your line out of the water and just walking away.

Describe a time when you experienced a prolonged wait that caused you to want to quit just so you wouldn't have to wait anymore.

What did you learn from that decision? Did you overcome your desire to quit and decide to hang in there instead? What were the results?

Most of us are like the prophet Habakkuk in times of waiting. We moan, whine, fuss, and complain. Even at God Himself. Habakkuk accused God of not hearing him at all. We read in Habakkuk 1:2, "How long, O Lᴏʀᴅ, will I call for help, And You will not hear?"

God's response to His servant doesn't offer much by way of comfort. We see it in the next chapter:

> Then the Lᴏʀᴅ *answered me and said,*
> *"Record the vision*
> *And inscribe it on tablets,*
> *That the one who reads it may run...*
> *For the vision is yet for the appointed time;*
> *It haŝtens toward the goal and it will not fail.*
> *Though it tarries, wait for it;*
> *For it will certainly come, it will not delay."*
> HABAKKUK 2:2-3

God promises the prophet the vision will not fail, but He also lets him know "it tarries." He reminds him to "wait for it." He doesn't tell him how long. He doesn't give him a sign. He just says it will one day come, so wait.

Read James 5:11. Would does this passage reveal that God will supply when we wait well?

Describe a situation in your life where it would look differently if you were to "remain steadfast" rather than responding in impatience, complaining, or doubt. What would change?

Isaiah 40:31 is a familiar verse to many people, but I do not want you to miss the powerful truths contained in it. Read it closely. List the four things that will happen if you wait well on the Lord.

1.

2.

3.

4.

We looked at Psalm 130:5-6 earlier, but let's return to it in order to dig deeper into what it reveals. When David refers to a watchman waiting for the morning, list some of the common emotions and expectations the watchman would be having as he waits.

1.

2.

3.

4.

5.

David tells us in this passage that we are to wait like the watchman does. We are to wait with hope that the morning will come or our answer will come. We are to wait with anticipation that what we expect to take place based on God's Word and what He has revealed to us will actually take place. We are to wait faithfully and obediently. Consider what would happen if the watchman decided to go to sleep and to no longer wait. The morning would come, but he would not be awake to receive it. In fact, he would get awakened by someone else and promptly removed from his job. Friend, you want to be awake when it is time for your destiny to reach you. You want to be alert, ready, energized, and fully engaged. You have waited this long—don't give up now. God may "tarry" with your change, outcome, or destiny, but He will deliver. Joseph had to wait years upon years until the dream he had of his brothers bowing down before him actually came true.

Read Genesis 37:9. Summarize the anticipated outcome of this verse in your own words.

Read Genesis 42:6. Compare what happened in this verse to Joseph's dream.

It would be twenty-two years between the time Joseph had his dream and the time that dream came true. That's twenty-two years. Not twenty-two days, or twenty-two months, and certainly not twenty-two minutes. Twenty-two years is a long time to wait for something. But what we see from Joseph's life and his eventual position of bringing hope, food, and life to starving nations, it was twenty-two years well spent in preparing for such an important destiny.

Read 1 Samuel 2:8. What is your initial reaction to this verse?

Is there any limit to what God can do to/for someone who is fully committed to Him?

In what ways can you be more committed to God and more trusting of His delays?

God's plan for you is a perfect plan. The destiny He has created you to fulfill is rewarding and significant. I know this because I know Him. God made you on purpose and for a purpose, but part of living out all God has in store involves waiting. It could be that you are waiting for other things outside of you to be in alignment with God's plan before He will bring it about. Or perhaps you have some more development to do. Or it could be a combination of both. Notice that when Joseph eventually did stand before Pharaoh to interpret the dreams, he no longer spoke as the young boy once did with great pride. He had been humbled through his experiences and in his humility; he had learned to not only depend more greatly on God but to also give the glory to God. There are a number of reasons why God delays, and we will not always be privy to what these reasons are. That's why the secret to waiting well is faith.

Prayer

Heavenly King, increase my faith so that I can wait on You
in a way that pleases You. Help me to not focus so much
on the future desire, goal, ambition, or even need that I
lose sight of the present. You are with me today. You have
a plan in place this very day. Help me to embrace today,
and each day, on this journey called life because You have
a purpose in the detours. In Christ's name, amen.

Day 3

COMPLAINING VERSUS CONTENTMENT

As we saw in the last two day's lessons, God is good to those who wait well. But what does it mean to wait well? How should we wait on the Lord in such a way that we receive His goodness at the end of it all?

There would be nothing worse than waiting for something and then not receiving the full reward because you balked, whined, and bailed along the way. Think about the Israelites wandering in the desert. Forty years is a long time to wait for anything. But, due to their sins, the original Israelites who fled slavery in Egypt weren't even able to enter into the promised land themselves—only those who came after them.

If you are going to have to wait on God's timing, development, and process, be sure to do it well, in a way that pleases Him and honors yourself. So what does that look like?

Does it mean to sit in a rocking chair and hope something better happens one day?

Does it mean to stop trying altogether?

When have you prayed enough?

When have you done enough?

When are you supposed to do nothing—or something?

None of those questions has an exact answer for each and every situation. The answer varies depending on the situation. But, overall, to wait on the Lord means to not go outside of God to fix or bring about the issue for which you are waiting. It means to not (as I call it) "pull an Abraham" and go find yourself a "Hagar" to try and usher in the promise yourself (see Genesis 16:1-4).

To wait on the Lord is to wait on His hand, His intervention, His guidance, His provision, His power, and His solution. It means to never try and force it into place. When it is God's time for you to fulfill your destiny, have the answer to your prayer, find resolution to your issue, etc. You will get there if you have waited well in faith.

Read Ephesians 2:10. What part of living out our purpose ("created for good works") depends on us, according to this verse?

What part depends on God?

Describe what it means to "walk in them" from Ephesians 2:10?

What emotions or feelings does it produce in you to know that you are not responsible for setting up your future or your purpose but rather to walk in it as God sets it up beforehand?

Now read Proverbs 19:21. In what way does this verse give insight into how tightly we should make (or hold) our plans?

You have heard of the endurance of Job and how God rewarded his patience through giving him twice of what he had before (Job 42:10). The Lord is full of compassion and mercy to those who will learn and practice the skill and art of waiting well.

Just as a farmer must wait for the rains and the soil to produce the growth of the seed, we must also wait for the Lord to produce within us and through us the purpose He intends.

Read James 5:7-8. Describe what actions or attitudes let us know that a farmer is waiting patiently for his crop to grow?

In what way can you apply these actions or attitudes to your own life?

I wasn't able to answer the questions at the start of this lesson on what it looks like to "wait well" because the answers vary based on the circumstances and people. But I can tell you what it doesn't look like. That one is easy. A lack of patience can be summed up in one word: complaining. A person who has a complaining spirit— someone who has a pattern of whining about their situation or about God—is not waiting well. Complaining reveals a lack of faith. Complaining reveals a heart seeking a solution more than the lesson on the journey to the solution.

Read Psalm 106:25. What was the result of the Israelites' complaining?

What are some areas in your life to which you can step up the application of the commandment in Philippians 2:14?

Read Genesis 40 again. When Joseph met with the baker and the cupbearer to interpret their dreams, in what way was his action a modeling of contentment?

What are some things we do (or don't do) when we are not content?

Read Numbers 11:1-4 and 1 Corinthians 10:10. In what ways does God allow "destruction" in our lives today as a result of our complaining?

As we saw in Psalm 106:25, the Israelites' complaining led to their disobedience as well. Complaining has a way of doing that. We work ourselves up so much in our mind and in our words that we eventually feel we need to take matters into our own hands and solve it ourselves. Yet, when that happens, we have just added our very own detour onto God's detour.

Scripture is replete with examples of people delaying the deliverance of their destiny because they tried to get there on their own. Abraham and Sarah had to wait twenty-five years before the promise of a child. The delay came because they went to the flesh to solve a situation of the spirit. Martha and Mary had to wait as Jesus intentionally delayed performing the miracle of raising their brother from the dead because their doubts, and subsequent faith, would be used to teach others for years to come. One of the surest ways to bringing about a swifter end to your detour is to trust God, be grateful in all things, and stop complaining. The reverse of that is true as well.

Prayer

God, I choose to surrender my situation to You. Help me to guard my mouth and keep it free from complaining. Let the meditation of my heart and the words from my lips please You, benefit others, and speak life into my everyday scenarios. Forgive me for when I have been impatient, for when I have complained, and for when I have lacked faith. In Christ's name, amen.

Day 4

DO WHAT YOU KNOW

When you are sick, you go to the doctor, and if she finds an infection, she writes you a prescription. Guess what the doctor expects you to do in your pain while you are waiting to get better? Take medicine. She doesn't expect you to read about the medicine. She doesn't expect you to talk about the medicine. She doesn't even expect you to understand what the medicine is and how it works. Just take the medicine and let it work. Just do what the doctor told you to do, and let the outcome present itself in time. When you or I take medicine, we wait for it to work. It is never instant.

But keep in mind, the longer you put off taking the medicine, the longer it will take for the medicine to work. And, if you choose not to take the medicine at all, you can pretty much expect to remain sick.

Far too many Christians like to talk to other people about what God's Word says we are to do in our lives. We like to think about His Word. Consider it. But far too many will actually act on it—put it into practice.

And yet, God, the Great Physician, has prescribed what we need in His Word. Whether or not we follow what He has revealed—things like love, forgiveness, trust, faith, hope, and more—will determine how long it takes for us to wait. These are the things being developed within us on detours. These are the characteristics of Christ.

Have you or someone you know ever delayed taking medicine for a sickness? What was the result?

Why do you think it takes longer for the body to heal when we delay taking the medicine designed to address the bacteria or symptoms in us?

In what ways can failure (or refusal) to live obediently to God, according to His revealed will in His Word, delay our deliverance, personal healing, and even our exit from a detour?

So, what am I to obey, you may be asking? You are to obey what you know. We are to obey what God has already revealed to us in His Word. You or I will never see what God plans to do in secret unless He sees us obeying what He has already revealed in public.

God never tells you everything He is going to do or what He wants you to do all at once. But, He has told you something. Whatever that is, obey it. However small, however insignificant it may seem—obey it. Do what you know to do even if you don't know what it is doing.

If you still don't know where to start, you can start with the simplest of all commandments to remember—but the most difficult to live out. I say it's simple to remember because it basically boils down to one word: love. I say it's difficult to live out because this one word contains the essence of all the other commandments we've ever been given (Matt. 22:37-40; Gal. 5:14). It says:

> *Love the Lord your God with all your heart, and with*
> *all your soul, and with all your strength, and with*
> *all your mind; and your neighbor as yourself.*
> LUKE 10:27

In what areas of your life do you feel you can improve in this area of loving God and loving others?

Is there something God has asked you to do that falls under this umbrella of love, but you have been hesitant or resistant to do it?

Are you willing to step out in faith and do the things you know God is asking you to do based on this commandment of love? (It's not important that you see the connection between your obedience and God's deliverance—the "how" is always worked out by God Himself.)

Read Job 42:10. What did Job do before he received a double portion from the Lord?

If you are unfamiliar with the story of Job, you will need to know that Job's friends were not that friendly to him at all. In fact, when Job was at the worst of times, his friends judged, griped, criticized, accused, and more. For Job, praying "for his friends" involved a lot more than asking God to bless those he loved and considered dear. It involved a significant amount of forgiveness, acceptance, humility, and love. It also involved faith.

It wasn't until after Job showed grace and kindness to those who had brought him pain during his greatest moments of pain that God restored him. This is because Job had obeyed the law of love and asked God to give His goodness to others. When Job did that, God gave goodness to Job as well.

Is there anyone in your life who is not easy to pray for or ask God's blessing over? Will you show them love by committing to pray for them every day for thirty days? If that commitment is too much right now, do what you can.

Who among your family and friends has effectively modeled unconditional love for you? What have you learned by observing them and their relationship with God?

Read Hosea 12:6. What are the three things we are to do based on this passage?

1.

2.

3.

Learning to wait well with patience involves learning how to put into practice the regularity of living as a child of God. It means putting into practice those things we already know.

FORGIVING.
LOVING.
BELIEVING.
WORKING as unto the Lord, even if it's not your favorite place to work.
HONORING the authority over you, even if you don't
particularly like or respect that authority.
BEARING with one another's burdens, even when
you feel weighted down by your own.

Do what God has already said to do. Then watch Him usher you straight out of your detour and into your destiny.

Prayer

Heavenly Father, I want to love like You love, forgive like You forgive, and honor You with my heart in every way. Mold me into the person You will take great pleasure in. Use me as a testimony of grace, kindness, and love to those around me. I pray for a double portion of favor and blessing in my life, God, and ask You to give me wisdom on how to set myself up for just that. In Christ's name, amen.

Day 5
TIME TO GROW

My son Anthony came home from school one day with an assignment. This assignment involved planting a seed in a small pot, watering it, and watching it grow. It was an assignment for his science class. Anthony dutifully put his seed in the soil in the pot on Friday night then went about his normal play and evening business. When he woke up on Saturday, he ran to the window to look at the pot. Nothing had happened. Nothing had grown. Anthony came to me disappointed because the seed had yielded nothing overnight.

I had to explain to Anthony that this wasn't one of Jack's magic beans which would grow into a vine reaching to the heavens overnight. This was a seed. And as with all seeds, it would take time to grow. It would require waiting, in faith. Watering, in faith. Watching, in faith.

When you plant a seed and wait for it to grow—or when you put a pot of water on the stovetop and wait for it to boil—is it best to stand there and watch it? Why not?

What are some ways you can learn how to wait well on the detours of life by applying principles you already employ when planting a seed or boiling some water?

Read Colossians 3:12. What are three truths about you from this passage.

1.

2.

3.

How should knowing these three truths, and resting in them, give you a greater ability to have patience in waiting on God's timing?

Have you ever witnessed in hindsight God having woven together a combination of things into one intended purpose that was difficult to discern as it was actually happening? What did you learn from this?

How can this experience strengthen your heart to wait in any current or future detours you may face?

Waiting does involve time. I'm sorry to have to stick with that truth, but it's true. So, the sooner we accept it as true, the sooner we can learn to do it well. To have patience requires something to be patient about.

When it's time for God to move in your life, it doesn't take long, but you must keep tending to your own soil and soul as you wait on Him to work out all He is doing on your detours. When God is silent, He is not still.

Prayer

Dear Lord, I choose to believe Your Word. I choose
to believe You are working all things out behind the
scenes for my good and Your glory. Help me to wait in
such a way that honors You, and give me signs of Your
goodness along the way. In Christ's name, amen.

Week 4

THE PARDON OF *DETOURS*

Start

Welcome everyone to session 4 of Detours.

Think about your personal study last week. What was a helpful point of review or a new insight you gained from it?

What new stories or updates related to our discussion and application from the previous group session does anyone have for us?

In this session we'll turn our attention to the pardon of detours.

When have you seen someone carry unforgiveness long after the fault occurred? How was that person affected?

Many of us carry around the burden of unforgiveness. We cling to hurts we cannot forget and imprison ourselves in a prison of circumstances. The sin of unforgiveness hinders us from getting to where God wants us to go. Today, Dr. Evans will discuss forgiveness and the freedom that comes from it when we pardon those we are blaming for our detours.

Before we see what Dr. Evans has to teach us about forgiveness, would somebody pray for our time together, asking the Lord to open our hearts and minds to His Word during our time together?

Watch

Complete this viewer guide as you watch the video for session 4.

One of the great hindrances of getting where God wants us to go is the
_____sin_____ of _____unforgiveness_____

Forgiveness is the ___decision___ to no longer credit and ___offense___
against the ___offender.___

Don't mistake the hand of ___God___ for the hand of ___Man___.

Two kinds of forgiveness:

  ___unilateral___ forgiveness

  ___transactional___ forgiveness

Transactional forgiveness starts with a ___Private___ ___Meeting___ not a
___Public___ ___Shared___.

God has a bigger ___program___ than your ___problem___.

Forgiveness does not only release the ___offender___; forgiveness releases
___you___.

Unforgiveness ___blocks___ what God wants to do for ___you___.

Forgiveness is a beautiful word, until you have to ___give___
___it___.

Respond

Discuss the video with your group, using the questions below.

Do you agree with Dr. Evans's definition of forgiveness? Why or why not?

What would you add to his definition of forgiveness?

Dr. Evans said that forgiveness does not necessarily mean that reconciliation will occur. How does this statement encourage you, or do you think some might say it seems like an excuse to not forgive?

On a scale of 1 to 10, how difficult is it for you to forgive someone who has wronged you? Do you have another scale of what offenses are more forgiveable than others?

How does knowing that forgiveness is a decision that doesn't necessarily require the emotion behind it, enable you to forgive more freely, to do the right thing?

How do you react to the statement, "Don't mistake the hand of God for the hand of man"? How does this statement change your perspective of conflict?

How have you seen God use the "ugly things" that have happen to you in your own detour process?

Dr. Evans said, "Forgiveness does not only release the offender; forgiveness releases you." Share with the group when you have experienced the freedom that comes from forgiveness.

Is there someone you need to release in biblical forgiveness? Has a name or a situation come to mind?

Read week 4 and complete the activities before the next group session.

Pardon and Unforgiveness

Unforgiveness. Bitterness. Resentment. Regret. Languishing over the loss of the past. All of these things, and those other things similar to them, hinder us from reaching our destiny. They keep us trapped on detours for far too long. They weigh heavy on us, causing our shoulders to slump and our smiles to turn downward.

Far too many people are failing to reach their destinations because they are still feeling loaded down by the pain of the past. The weight of yesterday continues to weigh them down today, keeping them from moving freely into tomorrow.

Nothing, and I mean nothing, will hinder you arriving at your destiny like this thing called unforgiveness. Unforgiveness includes holding on to past pain, past hurts, past grudges—the weightiness of regret, remorse, and revenge. Unforgiveness is that one thing above all else that will block God's movement in your life taking you from where you are to where you are supposed to go.

When you hang on to the weight of yesterday, it will hinder the progress to tomorrow.

Unforgiveness is that critical area that must be addressed if you are going to reach your destiny.

If anyone had a right to be angry, bitter, and hold a grudge, it was Joseph. But Joseph chose another path. Joseph chose another approach. He chose a different perspective.

If you and I want to be set free from unforgiveness, Joseph's perspective on pardon must be our own.

Day 1
THE WEIGHT OF YESTERDAY

If anyone had a right to not forgive what was done to him, it was Joseph.

Joseph grew up in a dysfunctional family under a dysfunctional father, was dumped in a pit, sold into slavery, unjustly jailed, and then forgotten. If anyone had a right to be angry and to say, "Life is not fair!" it was Joseph.

God gave so much of the first book of the Bible to Joseph because He wanted to show us the key components to living a life of destiny (Gen. 37–50). God wanted us to learn from this man. He wanted us to focus on this man's life lessons.

One of those critical components that Joseph had to grapple with is forgiveness. Biblical forgiveness is the decision to no longer credit an offense against an offender with a view of enacting vengeance. It also involves releasing that person from a debt owed as well as the blame that he or she deserves due to an infraction or sin committed against you.

Keep in mind, forgiveness is a decision. It is not first and foremost an emotion. It's not about how you are feeling at any given moment but rather about the choice you have made to no longer credit an offense or blame against an offender, even if that offender was yourself.

Read 1 Corinthians 13:5. How does this verse describe forgiveness?

According to this passage, does it mean that we are to ignore or forget wrongs done against us? What is it saying we are to do and not to do?

Read Psalm 130:3. In what way does this passage give insight into 1 Corinthians 13:5?

Do you think God forgets our sins in the literal interpretation of that word? Or, does He not count it against us? How are the two different?

Joseph's response toward those who had hurt him and had done him wrong is a good example for us. His response to his brothers lets us know that he had not grown emotionally cold. He had not chosen a life of cynicism in dealing with the pain he faced.

He still allowed himself to feel, despite the losses that had occurred in his life. He hadn't cut off the past. Rather, he had learned how to view it. He had learned how to accept it in alignment with God's providence, even though the pain was obviously still there.

Forgiveness doesn't mean you no longer feel pain. Nor does it mean to forget the facts about what happened. Forgiveness means you no longer hold the situation or person hostage for the pain that they caused. Joseph had to face it. He had to deal with it.

Read Genesis 50:15-17. What do Joseph's emotions reveal to us about his heart?

What are some dangers of unforgiveness with regard to a person's heart? I'll give you the first example: coldness.

Why does Satan seeks to remove positive emotions such as warmth, love, and compassion from our hearts through unforgiveness, resentment, and pain?

In counseling I have come across numbers of people who say that they have forgiven but their actions and words tell me—and those around them—otherwise. Their hearts are cold. Their words are sharp. Their patience is thin. Forgiveness is necessary because it enables you to be free and to love according to God's definition of love.

List two areas where you have struggled to forgive someone over the course of your lifetime.

1.

2.

What ways has this lack of forgiveness overflowed into your heart, trust, empathy, love, and in other ways?

Can you see how carrying around bitterness or resentment can affect you in other areas of your life?

Unforgiveness will impact not only yourself but also those around you—whether you intend it to or not. This happens due to the build-up of bitterness, the accumulation of a lack of trust, anger, and hate. The atmosphere that surrounds you and how you interact with others begins to be filled with the fumes of unforgiveness.

Maintaining healthy relationships becomes a challenge when you carry around the results of unforgiveness. Small offenses can get blown up into much more than they were, or you can withhold love and kindness whether in words or actions as a result of a hardened heart.

Friend, when you carry the weight of yesterday, it will ruin today. And if you ruin today, you will destroy tomorrow.

Prayer

Lord, thank You for reminding me through the life of Joseph that forgiveness is an option. I do not have to be bound by resentment, bitterness, or regret. God, I ask that You will strengthen my resolve to forgive and let go of pain and regret. Flood my heart with Your love and let that love overflow into me and onto others. I trust in Your sovereign hand. In Christ's name, amen.

Day 2

THE LEASH OF RESENTMENT

Many of us are being hindered from our destiny because we are being held hostage by a leash around our souls called unforgiveness. This leash keeps jerking us back and jerking us back. We take one step forward only to be jerked backed two. Maybe it was something that happened in your childhood, or maybe it was an abusive or emotionally-absent mate.

Maybe you were forsaken, neglected, or even wrongly demoted or let go. It could be a multitude of things. Whatever it is, though, it's holding you hostage. Isn't it time you were set free?

Did you know that the word used for forgiveness in the Bible is actually a math term, technically speaking? That's why when we hear it in the Lord's Prayer, it is specifically connected to "debts." We are asking God to forgive our debts as we forgive our debtors. It refers to an error in calculation, where two numbers have been added wrongly and you have to recalculate or erase in order to begin again.

Read Matthew 6:12. What does this verse mean to you?

In what way does refusing to forgive others impact God's relational forgiveness to you, according to this passage?

Forgiveness has far more to do with a decision than a feeling. It is not how you feel at any given moment. It has to do with whether you have made the choice to delete the offense. You may wonder how you are to know if you have made that choice since you can't gauge your decision by your feelings.

An excellent qualifying measure to help you know whether you have truly forgiven the offense and the offender is to ask yourself—are you still seeking revenge? If you are seeking revenge or payback, or you internally delight in the offender's pain or bad circumstances, then you have not yet forgiven. You have not yet released this person from the pain he or she has caused you.

Keep in mind, this also applies to you forgiving yourself. Far too many believers live under the weight of guilt and shame and fail to forgive themselves. This can lead to destructive behavior that can span the distance from overspending to overeating to overdrinking to other methods of self-harm.

True forgiveness is setting yourself free from the bitterness of wrath and anger. If you are seeking revenge or desiring it, then forgiveness has not occurred because love "does not keep a record of wrongs," (1 Cor. 13:5, HCSB).

Have you ever thought you had forgiven someone only to later take delight in something negative that happened to them? If so, what did that internal delight reveal about your true state of forgiveness?

Do you think God takes delight in our pain because He holds a grudge against us for things we have done to Him? How do you think God feels when we harbor ill feelings toward those we have been commanded by Him to forgive?

Read 2 Corinthians 1:3. In what way are we to model the heart of God in our own relationships?

Is it possible to give comfort and show mercy to someone you have failed to forgive? Why or why not?

I often compare the effect of sin in our lives—either done to us or done by us—to a wound or a cut on the soul. As with all wounds, if that is left untreated, it will simply fester and rot and become a place where bacteria has freedom to flourish.

I'm sure you have seen a cut that wasn't cared for. In time it oozed with puss and inflammation. Even the slightest brush against it caused significant pain.

Wounds of the soul are no different. When left untreated, they fill up with things like bitterness, regret, envy, jealousy, resentment, self-loathing, hate, and more. As all of this rises to the surface of our soul causing inflammation in our hearts, even the slightest offense against us can bring about great pain. We often call this overreacting. This is when a slight offense provokes a large response.

Identify a time in your life when you allowed unforgiveness to fester and rot, or someone else you know allowed this to happen in his/her life. Were there any overreactions to life's circumstances as a result?

Read Matthew 18:21-35. Pay particular attention to verses 34 and 35. What does this passage say will happen to you if and when you choose not to forgive?

The man in this parable who chose not to forgive was literally thrown in a jail and tortured. Similarly, when we choose not to forgive, our own hearts and souls and minds become a jail cell of resentment and personal torture. To live in this state of mind creates a cesspool of sin within us that ushers in "torture"—whether it be in our relationships, career, self-worth, or more.

Forgiveness is a command. When we are disobedient to this command, we are questioning the sovereignty of our all-powerful God and King. We are holding others to a higher standard than He has held for us. As a result, we will remain in the pit of our detours and in the company of our own pain.

Prayer

Dear Father, open my eyes to those areas in my life where bitterness and refusal to forgive are anchored like boats in a marina. Lord, please do not let me hold someone else to a standard that is higher than the one to which You have held me. You, through the death of Your sinless Son, Jesus Christ, have forgiven me of all of my sins. Help me to tap into the depth and strength of Your grace to do likewise for others who have hurt me. I know You can and will use all things to work together for good when I live according to Your purposes and trust Your plan. In Christ name, amen.

Day 3
UNILATERAL FORGIVENESS

Forgiveness can operate on two levels—unilateral forgiveness and transactional forgiveness. Unilateral forgiveness occurs when you forgive someone and yet the person has not asked for it, requested it, or even repented of what that person did to you. Unilaterally means that on your own—without his or her involvement—you choose to grant forgiveness.

List some reasons why you think you should grant unilateral forgiveness even though the person didn't ask for it and may not have even said he or she was sorry.

Read Acts 7:54-60. Describe how Stephen's request for forgiveness illustrates the concept of unilateral forgiveness.

Also, read Luke 23:34. What is one reason Jesus gave for asking for forgiveness toward others even though they did not ask to receive it?

In what ways should we seek to model our own forgiveness toward others after both Stephen and Jesus?

The reason you grant unilateral forgiveness is so that you can keep going. Unilateral forgiveness keeps you from being held hostage to something the other person may never get right. It could be that the offense is so small that it is not a big deal to the other person, or it's so small you don't want to bring it up. Maybe the person who hurt you has passed away and the opportunity for apologizing is no longer available. Perhaps, it may be that the person who hurt you refuses to be repentant or even fails to see what he or she did wrong.

Have you ever offered unilateral forgiveness to someone? What impact did that have on your own well-being?

Is there someone you need to forgive unilaterally? Will you take a moment to pray, asking God to help you to do this?

Never let the fact that people who have hurt you have neither asked for forgiveness or even demonstrated that they deserve it keep you from giving it. You are to forgive so that you are no longer held hostage to an offense, person, circumstance, or loss. By an act of your decision, you release them so that you can keep going to your destiny. Nothing will hold you hostage to your detours and thus keep you from your destiny like unforgiveness.

Revisit Acts 7:54-60. Pay particular attention to verses 55 and 56. What special experience did Stephen receive by having a heart bent toward forgiveness?

Have you ever experienced God in an intimate way due to your willingness to forgive? Can you share what that was like? If you have not, are you willing to forgive at a greater level so that you can deepen your relationship with the Lord?

Read Matthew 5:11-12. Describe how this verse relates to the effect of forgiveness in our lives and directly in our relationship with God.

I want to tell you one very important thing about unilateral forgiveness. It doesn't stop the pain from showing up in your life. What hurt you caused pain and it will take time to heal. Joseph's emotions were real as he wept before his brothers so many years later. What unilateral forgiveness does do is allow you to put the pain in the proper perspective. It allows you to distance yourself from the offense enough for the natural momentum of life and emotions to finally slow down and eventually rest so they are no longer triggered so easily. The pain will subside in time, as long as you don't pick the resentment back up again.

Leave vengeance in the hands of God. He's far better at it than we are anyhow. Give yourself the freedom you so desperately need and so divinely deserve that will enable you to fully live out the destiny you have been created to fulfill. Forgive. Let go. Embrace the truth that God's perfect plan involves the pain of the past, and He will bring it to His good purpose.

Read Deuteronomy 32:35 and Romans 12:19. What do these two verses tell you about God's ability, and even desire, to right wrongs?

In what area of your life do you need to let go and allow God the freedom to bring about justice on your behalf?

Forgiveness is a beautiful word when you need it. It is an ugly word when you have to give it. But, it is a bridge we all must cross, and it is certainly a bridge we should never burn down. Forgive others because you also need forgiveness, from God and those you offend (Matt. 6:14-15).

Prayer

Loving God, it is easy to hold a grudge and hang onto bitterness, especially when I truly have been wronged and the person who did it does not feel or demonstrate remorse. Lord, it is in times like these that I must trust You. I must believe that You are a judge and you do right wrongs if I will let go of my anger and unforgiveness. Please, God, show up for me in this area—You know what it is—and let me see Your hand of vindication and justice. Let me witness the power of forgiveness as it was so clearly demonstrated in Joseph's life. In Christ's name, amen.

Day 4
MAKING MOUNTAINS MOVE

Sometimes getting stuck on a detour might feel as overwhelming as if you are standing in front of a mountain that blocks your way. No matter how hard you try, you cannot seem to find a way to go over, around, or through the mountain. Jesus had something important to say about mountains in our lives, and surprisingly, it has to do with forgiveness.

List three things you are facing in your life (relationships, work, personal emotions, etc.) that feel like unmovable mountains.

1.

2.

3.

Take a look at Mark 11:22-24. According to verse 23, what do you need in order to move mountains in your way?

Faith the size of a mustard seed is enough to uproot a tree and cast it into the sea (Luke 17:6). Belief without doubt is enough to move a mountain. Both of these principles are ones we hear often when people or preachers talk about solving issues in life. But there is another all-important truth tied to this that is too often overlooked by many.

Read Mark 11:25-26. What does Jesus say we are to do when we are praying? What happens if we do not do it?

For God to be free to enable and empower you to move the mountains you are facing in your life today, and in your future, you must forgive. Moving mountains hinges upon the purity of your relationship with God. The purity of that relationship hinges on this one thing called forgiveness. If anything blocks the flow of God's power in your life more than all else, it is unforgiveness.

However, sometimes God doesn't choose to move the mountains in our lives. Sometimes He gives us the strength to go around them or over them. Many of you are familiar with the classic children's story *The Little Engine That Could*. It's a tale about a little train engine who, through the power of belief ("I think I can. I think I can."), pulls an unbelievable load up a mountainside. It has endured for over a century because so many of us connect with it; we want to be that engine.

Yet, if we're honest, many of us actually relate better to those greater, bigger engines that are unable to pull the load up the hill. They convince themselves that the load is too big and that they can't do it. Similarly, we face our own personal challenges with such disbelief. We approach seemingly impossible detours that only go on and on, such as trying to lose weight or getting out of debt by looking at the size of the problem and becoming disheartened. "I'll never lose all this weight." "I'll never pay that off."

So, what's that little engine's secret? Why is he able to go up the mountain? As I see it, he has two things going for him. First, he thinks he can. It's as simple as that. He truly believes in his heart that, regardless of the size of the load, he can actually get it up the hill. Second, he focuses more on where he's going than on where he's been. The little engine doesn't get caught up in the myriad of things that can bring him down and rather looks ahead at the goals instead.

Unforgiveness keeps you looking back because that is the only direction you can see. When you do not forgive, your mind stays stuck in the past. This is because the events or words of the past are what consume your thoughts and attention. You cannot simultaneously look out the front windshield of a car and its rearview mirror. You must choose. Forgiveness is choosing to stop focusing on the past and start believing in a better tomorrow.

Read Luke 6:37-38. In what way does your lack of forgiving others come back on you?

In what way does doing good to others return to you?

Write down two people/situations where you will choose to do good rather than harbor unforgiveness. Be intentional and ongoing about doing something good in both of these situations and watch how God responds.

Choosing to forgive opens up the opportunity for God to do amazing things both in you and through you. Nothing models the heart of Jesus Christ more than a heart of forgiveness. Joseph modeled this for us in his life.

Read Genesis 50:20. What overarching truth enabled Joseph to forgive?

Have you seen God turn something someone else meant for harm in your life into good? Share how this came about. Did witnessing this help you to forgive?

If you've spent your life stuck on detours or blocked by mountains, consider the role forgiving can play in setting you free and ushering you into your destiny. Take some time to do a personal inventory on any bitterness, resentment, or anger you are still holding onto. Ask God to give you the power, wisdom, and insight necessary to release this and allow love to replace it through forgiveness.

Prayer

Lord, I want to be filled with a heart of love, not only for other's sake but for my own. I realize how challenges I face may be as a result of my own relational distance from You, the result of unforgiveness and a lack of faith. God, I surrender these emotions to You as a decision to forgive _____. Flood me with Your peace and let me experience the overwhelming power of Your presence in my life and in my life challenges. In Christ's name, amen.

Day 5
TRANSACTIONAL FORGIVENESS

Let's take a moment to review what we've covered this week. First, we looked at how forgiveness is not an emotion but rather it is a decision. Biblical forgiveness is the decision to no longer charge an offense against an offender with a view of enacting vengeance. It also involves releasing that person from a debt owed as well as the blame that he or she deserves due to an infraction or sin that has been committed against you.

Secondly, we saw how allowing wounds of hurt, bitterness, and anger to fester can cause us to lash out at others when they trigger these wounds, even through something slight. We also saw how we can offer forgiveness to someone who is not sorry or is not able to be sorry due to circumstances through unilateral forgiveness. Both Jesus and Stephen gave us examples of this as they died. Lastly, we looked at how forgiveness can cause distance in our relationship with God and thus hinder our ability to not only see Him but to have faith in Him to such a degree that enables us to overcome life's challenges, sometimes referred to mountains in Scripture.

Name some personal benefits to choosing forgiveness when others have caused you pain.

In what way does allowing unforgiveness in your life prevent you from reaching your destiny?

For our final day on this subject, we are going to look at another type of forgiveness—transactional forgiveness. This happens when someone is truly sorry for what they have done to you, expresses their sorrow to you, and you choose to forgive. It is two-directional forgiveness rather than one-directional only, such as in unilateral forgiveness. It also will often involve seeking to restore what has been damaged by the one who damaged it.

What can make the process of transactional forgiveness difficult to carry out is the inability to directly discern the authenticity of the repentance. It could be that the motivation is pure and that he or she is truly repentant, but then again it could be simply because that person got caught and is trying to avoid the consequences.

Have you ever given or experienced transactional forgiveness? Explain the impact of this experience on your relationship with that person.

It's important in situations where you are offering transactional forgiveness to test the fruit of repentance. This is similar to what Joseph did when his brothers asked him to forgive them in Egypt.

Read Genesis 42:15-16. How did Joseph seek to "test" his brothers?

In this passage, Joseph stated that he was testing whether or not his brothers were telling the truth. At that time, his brothers weren't aware that this was their brother they had lied about and sold into slavery. But Joseph was aware of what they had done to him twenty-two years before and because of that, he sought to test their hearts and character to see if they had changed or had remained the same as they had been.

Voicing your repentance through an apology is one thing. But if those words are not backed up by a change in your actions—"the fruit of repentance"—the words may simply be said with a wrong motive. True repentance leads to life; remorse leads to death—whether a death in a relationship, situation, emotions, or even life.

Read Luke 22:62. What did Peter's sorrow lead him to do?

When people seek transactional forgiveness from you, it is important to clearly see through time, words, and actions that it is true repentance they are offering, and not just remorse, before you restore the relationship. It is important to see that they have truly turned from the sin, or patterns of sin, they were committing against you. You are to forgive immediately, yes, but trust is rebuilt over time.

What are some ways to test the validity of someone's remorse when he/ she has hurt you in some way?

Describe the difference between forgiving and trusting.

Don't let the feelings of the pain get in the way of your forgiveness. Sometimes forgiveness is hard because we've been ringing the bell for so long that we don't know how life is without the bell. Sometimes we leave the bell alone for a while, but then we pick up the rope and start ringing it all over again. Forgiveness is an ongoing life decision because we are human and live with humans, and we all have sin natures.

Mastering the art of forgiveness will free you to fully live out your destiny like nothing else—because nothing else more accurately reflects the heart of our living God and Savior.

Prayer

Heavenly Father, thank You for modeling for me what it looks like to forgive. You forgive me for things time and time again, and yet I still hold onto bitterness toward others who have harmed me. Open my mind and my eyes to see Your hand orchestrating and allowing all things to happen for an intended purpose of good. Let that truth strengthen my soul to forgive more freely and live with a pure love toward others, as Your love is toward me. In Christ's name, amen.

Week 5

THE PROMOTION OF
DETOURS

Start

Welcome everyone to session 5 of Detours.

What did you learn from your personal study last week? that has influenced or made a difference in your choices or thinking?

What can anyone share related to our discussion and application from the previous group session?

In this session we'll turn our attention to the promotion of detours, the idea that the change in route could prepare you for greater rewards or responsibilities..

Have you ever been forgotten? Left behind? Passed over? Share a recent example—funny or serious—of being forgotten.

Detours can often seem to linger, but they are certainly not forever. They are temporary, and we will graduate out of them when we are ready. When we are ready, the changes we have experienced may promote us to a better future. Today, Dr. Evans discusses the promotion of detours.

Before we see what Dr. Evans has to teach us, would somebody pray for our time together, asking the Lord to open our hearts and minds to His Word?

Watch

Complete this viewer guide as you watch the video for session 5.

Extraordinary trials demand an extraordinary _____ because there is an extraordinary _____.

It's time for your promotion when God does on your detour _____

_____ _____ _____ that you tried to do during your detour.

_____ is where God applies _____ to our specific situation.

Keep your _____ open for _____.

God does not limit Himself to _____ _____ to get us where He wants us to go.

Respond

Discuss the video with your group, using the questions below.

Using the illustration of an ironed shirt, Dr. Evans pointed out that heat, or discomfort, can shape us into something better. How has God used this figurative heat to shape you into something He can use for His glory?

Share an experience of when you knew your detour was truly over and that you were back on "the main highway."

Sometimes we think we are almost finished with a detour, then something happens to turn us back around instead of continuing on our planned way. Share with the group moments when you thought you were almost out of a detour but it ended up not being the end or rescue from a delay that you were hoping for.

What have you learned about the character of God and how He rescues us from detours?

What have you learned about God's timing through Joseph's story?

How have you seen God's timing in your experience with detours?

How have you seen God use a diversion in your life to take you to where you ought to be? Looking back, how did God use that time to develop you?

How can Joseph's detours encourage you while you're on your own detour?

Read week 5 and complete the activities before the next group session.

Meant for Your Destiny

Meant.

The word can be defined as the past participle of "to mean" which is to intend for a particular purpose and destination. You've probably heard someone say something they probably shouldn't have said or done something that lacked tact, but someone else tried to cover it up with, "They meant well." What they were saying is that even though what the person said or did created a negative reality, that was not their intention. They hadn't meant to cause harm.

But that was not the case with Joseph's brothers when they stripped him of his coat and dumped him in a pit. Nor was that the case when they greedily plucked him from the pit and sold him for a profit to slave traders headed to a foreign land.

Joseph's brothers meant anything but well. They meant to cause him harm. They meant to ruin his life. They meant to dethrone him from the position of importance he had come to believe he would one day hold. They meant to harm him. Actually, they meant evil.

But God.

Those two words are two powerful words. When you come across "but God" in Scripture, pay attention. What comes next will usually change the entire situation. Especially if "meant" is added after them.

But God meant ....

As we saw in last week's lesson on forgiveness, Genesis 50:20 shows what God can do with something meant to harm you. He can not only protect you in it, but He can also promote you because of it. The exact thing Joseph's brothers had meant to cause him harm was the exact thing God used to promote him to his destiny.

Day 1

DISAPPOINTMENT TO PROMOTION

Joseph's detour started when he was seventeen years old. By the time we reach Genesis 41, he's thirty years old. That's thirteen long years of wandering and waiting, not really knowing why God had allowed so many twists and turns along the way. It was a long detour, no doubt. But it had an exit. It had a destination. It had a purpose tied to the delays. It had an end to its untimely beginning. And from Joseph's example, we can pick up on some clues that can help us recognize when God is ready to bring us to the end of a detour.

The first of which is when God disappoints you just when you thought He was coming through for you.

I know you didn't expect to read that. You probably expected me to say something like when God gives you a glimpse of your destiny on the horizon and points you in the right direction, or something similar, but God doesn't work the way we want Him to sometimes.

A lesson from the life of Joseph with regard to detours is that just when it looks like God is about to deliver you, and He disappoints you instead, you are on your path to your ultimate promotion.

Write down a time when you felt God was going to come through for you, but He disappointed you instead. In hindsight, can you see how He used that disappointment to prepare you for your ultimate promotion?

How do you think Joseph felt when he was on the cusp of being released (after interpreting the two dreams of the fellow prisoners) but two long years went by and he realized he had been forgotten? Read Genesis 40–41:1 for the context in answering that question.

Have you ever had to wait longer than you originally thought you would? What are some thoughts and emotions you had during that time?

Do you think Joseph struggled with any of those similar thoughts or emotions? In what way?

To Joseph, it had looked like God had finally brought someone into his life who could help him and deliver him—someone who could give a good word for him. It looked like his day had finally arrived, but things went left before they ever went right. Things stalled before they ever took off. The cupbearer forgot Joseph. And Joseph had no way to get his attention again. I imagine it looked like to Joseph that God had disappointed him.

As bad as it may feel when God disappoints you, it is actually a great thing because He is setting you up for where He is taking you. He is getting you prepared—you are almost there. Just hang on a bit longer and don't throw in the towel just yet. He's strengthening your faith, gratitude, and resolve.

He's also preparing the place or person He is taking you to—for you.

That is something we don't always consider in our me-centered culture. Your destiny may not actually be ready for you yet. God may be preparing the place you are going or the person He is going to connect you with for you as well.

Read Hebrews 11:7. What would have happened if God would have instructed Noah to build the ark only as the rain began to fall? Or, what would have happened if Noah had built it too many years before the floods came, and it was left to sit and rot?

What do we learn from the lesson of Noah on God's perfect timing?

Have you ever considered how God may be preparing the thing/person you are waiting on in order to be ready for you? Maybe it's a future mate, a job, a dream—any number of things. What truths can you think on to help you wait with the right heart spirit?

How do all things need to be ready in order for the timing to be right for your promotion?

Joseph spent the bulk of his life waiting on God to promote him into his destiny. Joseph didn't even get to have his own family until he was well passed the years that men in his culture wed and had children. He didn't have a career with upward mobility either. After all, slavery and then a jail cell are usually pretty limiting when it comes to promotion. Joseph held no degrees. He was an outsider in a culture which was obsessed with their own culture. If anyone should have any reason to give up, throw in the towel, and just give in to a fatalistic mentality, it would have been Joseph.

But Joseph didn't give in. He kept showing up, day in and day out. We know this because Scripture tells us that the Lord was with Joseph and also granted him favor with those around him. We also know that God continued to promote him wherever he was to have greater authority and influence.

Promotion doesn't go to the one who tossed in the towel. Promotion usually goes to the one who is using that towel—and using it well, no matter how disappointed things may appear. This is because promotion is always a matter of timing. It's a matter of God setting up the intersections of life so that when you get there, the people you are connecting with are ready for you. And, even more importantly, you are ready to handle what has been given to you as well.

Read Psalm 105:16-19. Notice the phrase "until the time." What happened to Joseph until the time of his promotion?

How can you apply the truth of that reality to your own waiting?

One reason God has you waiting for your promotion to your destiny is because He is doing something bigger than you.

Yes, you are the one waiting, feeling the disappointment, lack, or desire, but what God is setting up involves more than just you. Like the strands woven together to create a tapestry of an image no single strand has the ability to display, we are all interlinked by God in His divine plan. You are one strand. Joseph was one strand in God's larger kingdom plan of preserving a family for the building of a nation.

As is often the case, the most important strands have to wait the longest and develop the most before being given their part to play. As you wait on the promotion into your destiny, realize that one of the reasons you are waiting is because God is up to something bigger than just you. He is setting up all sides of the equation before He connects them. Trust me, I've seen this in my own life—it is worth the wait.

Prayer

Jesus, thank You for what You are doing behind the scenes. Thank You for preparing me for the promotion to my destiny. I know that You are arranging things for the greater good of all involved. Help me to wait well. Help me to face disappointment with the anticipation that You are near and about to do something grand. Plant in me the seed of expectation knowing that You have a great plan and destination up ahead. In Christ's name, amen.

Day 2
SPIRITUAL GROWTH

Have you ever been traveling by airplane only to have the plane re-routed due to weather or other factors? Have you ever been on a plane and unable to land because the pilot has you in what is called a holding pattern?

Some of you going through this Bible study may feel like that's the story of your life. You planned to be somewhere by now and yet you are in a holding pattern. You don't know when the plane called destiny is going to land. Maybe you've been stuck on the tarmac of trials and tribulation and have even forgotten where you intended to go all along.

If this sounds familiar to you, please know that God has a purpose for your pain and a destination at the end of your detour. When your preparation meets God's purpose—when your time connects with His time—you are ready to move from detour to destiny.

Read Proverbs 3:5. How can you apply that verse to a situation you are waiting on God to intervene in or solve?

Always remember when looking at the detours in your life that God is crafting your destination while He is developing you. He is crafting a purpose while developing a person. When the person is prepared for the purpose and the purpose is prepared for the person, that is when God creates a connection.

The problem occurs when God has prepared the purpose, but the person is not yet ready for it. Then, you have this purpose dangling out there without a person ready to fulfill it. When the preparation has not been allowed to do its work in order to produce focus, maturity, character, and faith, it only lengthens the necessary detour.

Read Ephesians 4:14-15. Why is it important for you to grow to maturity in order to effectively carry out your destiny?

119

In what ways can Satan seek to divert or distract you from maturing in Christ? Consider ways particularly related to your destiny.

Read 1 Peter 3:8. What are you to grow in?

Growth takes time. And growth often takes trials. Unfortunately that is just the nature of growth. God sometimes has to allow something to break in us in order to align and strengthen us for our destiny.

For a plant to rise from the soil, the seed must be broken open by the substance inside. For a baby chick to experience life, it must break the egg that surrounds it. Even to enjoy the fragrance of a perfume, we must break the seal on the bottle that holds it. I understand that we as a culture are often scared of broken things. But I want you to know that God finds beauty in brokenness.

Complete humility before God is a form of brokenness that He values greatly. In fact, spiritual brokenness is such a critical component to maturity and effectiveness as a believer that far too many of us do not reach our destinies simply out of trying to avoid this thing called brokenness.

Simply stated, brokenness is the work of God by which He strips us of our pride and self-sufficiency so that the power of Christ works in and through us. Brokenness develops within us a dependence on God for all we do.

The fact is that many people have suffered catastrophes without drawing any closer to God or even acknowledging Him. The issue in brokenness is not so much the circumstances but our response to what God is teaching us through the circumstances He allows to come into our lives. Not everyone arrives at their destinies like Joseph did because not everyone responds to life's breaking by depending more fully on God.

Read Galatians 2:20. In your own words, what does it mean to be crucified with Christ?

According to Paul's writing in this verse, you're a dead person. Nevertheless, you're a living dead person because you are alive yet immortal through Jesus Christ, who lives within your mortal flesh. We could say you are a "dead man walking." What does this mean? It means that your dependence is entirely on God. You are to yield your will, desires, and even your ambitions to the Lord. There is nothing worse than a dead lamb on the altar seeking to climb right off, but that is exactly what many of us do in our relationship with God. And then we wonder why we cannot seem to get farther than we are in our Christian walk.

Read 2 Timothy 2:22. What are you to flee? Name what some of these might be in your life.

What are you to pursue?

In what way can you actively pursue these things?

God's promotion of you out of your detour and into your destiny often depends on your personal maturity. This is because in order for God to place you in your destiny only to have you squander your promotion on spiritual immaturity would be disastrous. Personal growth and surrender to God is essential to your personal use and promotion by God.

Prayer

Dear Lord, make me into a person You can use fully. Strengthen me in the virtues I need to be strengthened in. Prune me of the sins I must remove. Allow me the diligence to stand strong in the process You use as I am in the holding patterns of life. Make me fully committed to You in all things. And, for that, I thank You in advance in faith. In Christ's name, amen.

Day 3
BROKENNESS

Brokenness and humility are not popular topics to write on or read about, but they are critical to your promotion on your detour. If I did not share these principles with you, I would be negligent in teaching you the whole truth about this process called detours.

When you choose to avoid difficulties through distractions, or other coping mechanisms, rather than embracing them to help you grow, you take the "easy way out" but you also short-circuit the promotion on your detour.

The Bible is replete with the reality of brokenness and how God uses this humbling experience to strip us of our self-sufficiency. Let's read a few:

- Psalm 34:18: "The LORD is near to the brokenhearted and saves those who are crushed in spirit."
- Psalm 51:17: "The sacrifices of God are a broken spirit; a broken and a contrite heart, O God, You will not despise."
- Psalm 138:6: "For though the LORD is exalted, yet He regards the lowly, but the haughty He knows from afar."
- Isaiah 57:15: "For thus says the high and exalted One who lives forever, whose name is Holy, 'I dwell on a high and holy place, and also with the contrite and lowly of spirit in order to revive the spirit of the lowly and to revive the heart of the contrite.'"
- Isaiah 66:2: "But to this one I will look, to him who is humble and contrite of spirit, and who trembles at My word."

What are some major themes you pick up in those verses?

Re-write your favorite verse from the list above in your own words and apply it to your own life.

What happens as a result of brokenness and humility?

If you're a parent, you know how different your children are in the way they respond to discipline. One child will collapse in tears at the slightest word of correction. Another one may stand stubbornly despite all you do to try and correct him or her.

Paul was definitely in the latter category before his salvation. God had to discipline Saul severely until he was literally facedown in the dirt. Up to the moment of his conversion, Saul was self-righteous, self-sufficient, and a powerful force for evil in this world. But the moment Saul met Jesus, his independence ended, and he became totally dependent on the Lord. To reinforce to Saul the reality of his new dependent status, God struck him blind for three days, and he was totally dependent on others (Acts 9:8).

You and I need to know that God will do whatever it takes, for as long as it takes, to bring us to the point of true brokenness, dependence, and humility so that His will can be made manifest in us. We can help determine how long the process takes by our response, or resistance, to the process. We have a say in the length of our detours.

What is God trying to break in you to humble you? If there is no area currently, has there been one in the past? What was the result?

Read 1 Thessalonians 5:23. In what order does Paul say we are to be sanctified? Why do you think he chose this order?

In what way do our thoughts impact our actions?

The problem with a thief is not his hands. The problem with a drunk is not her mouth. The problem with a gossip is not the words he says. The problems we all deal with are rooted in our spirit and in our soul. That is why it is not as easy as changing your behavior to change your character. Brokenness and humility are done on the inside and often require a time of true humbling before they take root within you.

Read 2 Corinthians 12:9. What happens when we are broken, humbled, or weak?

Even though this is truth from the verse in the previous question, why do you (or why do people) often resist brokenness, humility, and weakness?

You may encounter any kind of trial in the process of being broken, but don't mistake the hand of man for the hand of God. Just as we have seen in the life of Joseph, God allows people, problems, and situations to achieve His will. Trying to run from problems by changing jobs or spouses may take you from the fire but only land you in the frying pan.

Sometimes God wants you to hit rock bottom so you will discover that He's the Rock at the bottom. He will do whatever it takes to bring you, like Joseph, to the place of brokenness and humility.

When I was a kid, I had one of those classic piggy banks with the coin slot in the top. When I wanted to get money out of the bank, there was only thing I could do—turn it upside down and shake it hard. I did a lot of shaking because there was something of value inside that I wanted to bring to the outside.

God does the same thing with us. We have a great treasure inside us, the Holy Spirit, but that treasure is encased in a hard shell that hides it. So God has to shake and strip us to bring the treasure out. Sometimes He even has to break us altogether to reveal the true value inside.

Prayer

Heavenly Father, give me the grace to stand up underneath
Your hand that allows humility to be developed in me.
Show me how to cooperate with Your will in my life and
give me the gift of brokenness so that I may be used by You
in all the ways You so desire. In Christ's name, amen.

Day 4
GOD PROVIDES THE EXIT

Detours are not random. They are not chance happenings which force you to slow down, re-evaluate, and look to God for a way out. Detours always come with a purpose. Much of that purpose has to do with waiting on God to set things up for your arrival. It will also include God developing you so that you are ready when you do arrive. Whatever the case, we can know for certain that the God who hung the stars in the sky is able to bring your detour to an end if He wanted to. So if you are still there, He still has a reason.

Read James 1:12. What two things happen in this verse?

1.

2.

In James 1:12, the man persevered under trial and the man receives a crown of life and blessing for persevering. The verse also goes on to say that God gives this gift to "those who love Him." How does love for God help you to persevere under trial?

According to John 14:15, what are we to do if we love Christ?

What are some of the commandments we are to keep, related to waiting on God in detours? If you don't know the exact verses, write down the overall theme of the commandments and verses.

In what way does viewing waiting on God and persevering in a trial as an act of loving God help make those actions more doable?

When I get up to go to work, I pick out an ironed shirt. The reason I do that is because if the shirt is not ironed, it's wrinkled. In order to get the wrinkles out, a little heat has to be put on a shirt. Now, whoever is ironing the shirt is not trying to be mean to my wardrobe. They are just making the shirt look good enough to wear in public.

When God sends you on a detour, He is not hating on you. He is not being mean to you. He is just making you ready because He wants to wear you as His representative. He wants to look good with you reflecting His image and His name.

Yes, the ironing process sometimes gets a little warm. It may even get a little bit uncomfortable. The steam of your pain rises at times, but it is only because God has a purpose and a plan for your life, and He is working on you and in you to perfectly carry out that purpose for Him.

Read Romans 12:12. What three things are we to do based on this passage?

1.

2.

3.

In what way do all three of these things weave together during a detour?

Extraordinary trials provide the opportunity for extraordinary preparation because they are leading to an extraordinary purpose. If you have been going through some rough things, life has been tough, and detours won't seem to leave you alone, just know that God is up to something great. God has got something commensurate with your pain as He takes you to your pinnacle.

We saw how Joseph was forgotten and had to play the waiting game. Joseph was forced to languish in uncertainty for an extended period of time. But when his wait was over, Joseph was promoted beyond what he could have ever hoped or even dreamed. God not only made a way out of no way to provide Joseph his freedom again; God gave Joseph power, authority, significance, and joy unlike many had ever experienced. God can do something similar with you if you will remain with Him in both heart and actions during your detours.

Read Mark 4:16-17. What is a common reaction to life trials and detours?

Read Mark 4:20. What is one thing you can do to help strengthen you not to fall away during trials and detours?

How do you know when you are getting close to exiting your detour and heading into your promotion? That would be when God does on your detour what you could never do on your own. During your detour you are trying to find you way to the main highway and simply trying to figure out what is going on. You are not able to get off the road you are traveling. God won't let you escape. But there finally comes a time when He shows you a sign—maybe it's a turn that opens up to the main highway, and you make it.

Often this is done through a way you had tried to do on your own before but were unsuccessful. Remember how Joseph tried to get the cupbearer to remember him? He asked him to remember him. He hoped he would remember him. But the cupbearer forgot him entirely. Only God did that precise thing a few years later. He caused the cupbearer to remember Joseph. God is the One who is in control. Detours teach us this more than anything.

Prayer

Father, I want to see Your deliverance on my detour and in this mess. I know that I have tried time and time again to find a way out, but You, Lord, are giving me a way out. I just can't see it yet. I choose then to trust in You, knowing that You can open up a way in no time at all. Thank You in advance for Your gracious exit and promotion for me out of this trial and time of testing. In Christ's name, amen.

Day 5
FULFILL YOUR DESTINY

This has been a great week of study, hasn't it? I love the lessons learned from the life of Joseph. His story provides a unique vantage point into this area of detours and waiting, unlike many others. At the beginning of our week's lesson, we looked at one of the ways you can know you are on a God-ordained detour. This was when you experience disappointment because you thought you had figured a way out yourself but the door slammed shut.

Joseph had interpreted the two men's dreams in jail and asked the cupbearer to remember him when he was set free. I imagine Joseph's heart felt the first pangs of hope again after so many years in jail. It could be that he kept his eyes on the jail cell door over the next few days, weeks, and months, waiting for the return of the cupbearer to thank him and release him. Yet, day after day, week after week, no one came. Being let down and disappointed is one thing. Being let down and disappointed when hope is on the horizon is another thing altogether. However, God had Joseph exactly where He wanted him. It just wasn't time for the fullness of Joseph's destiny.

Is it possible to have your hopes lifted, have them dashed, and still be on your God-ordained detour?

Read Psalm 39:7. When we are forced to wait on an answer, deliverance, or open door, where is the only place we are to put our hope?

After looking at Joseph's disappointment on day one of our lesson this week, we then turned our attention to what is accomplished prior to our promotion. For starters, we talked about the purpose of spiritual growth. God will frequently use a time of testing and trial in our lives to produce within us a new level of humility, brokenness, and dependence upon Him. We see how this was produced in Joseph because once he became promoted, he handled himself with grace and mercy in front of both Pharaoh and his brothers later on. God had to prepare Joseph's character for the great calling He had for him. His detours did just that.

Read Romans 8:24-25. How are we to wait during times of detours?

What area of your life could benefit from some more patience as you wait?

Have you ever experienced God promoting you after a time of trial, testing, or detour? In what way do you look back and see how you were developed in this time?

Brokenness is often the key to a breakthrough. God created you with a tremendous amount of spirit, will, drive, ambition, and desire. This is because you are made in the image of the almighty God. All of those things must be yoked and yielded underneath the Lordship of Jesus Christ for them to be useful rather than harmful toward God's overarching plan.

You may have seen on television or in a movie, or even in person, a wild horse who carried himself with great power. The horse was beautiful and strong. But until the horse was able to be "broken," the horse could never be of any benefit to the owner. The horse doesn't lose his strength during the breaking process. Rather, the horse learns how to use that strength for the good of all involved.

Give a biblical example of someone who was humbled and broken before God could use him/her more fully.

Read Genesis 32:22-32. What happened to Jacob as a result of wrestling with God?

If you are in the midst of a trying detour, have you turned to God like Jacob did and asked Him to bless you? Consider the power of humility and brokenness before the Lord and spend time with Him in prayer seeking His promotion out of your detour.

When the kids were growing up, we sometimes had Pop-tarts® in the house. Pop-tarts aren't as easy to get right as you may think. You push them down to warm them up but for some reason, it seems they would always pop up before they were quite done. You would hear the sound of the "pop" but when you reached to take it out of the toaster, it would be cool. Then you would have to push it back down

This simple illustration can help us remember that prior to our promotions on our detours, God is waiting to make sure we are perfectly ready. We may think we are ready or see a sign of an exit only to be pushed back in and told to wait some more. This is exactly what happened to Joseph, but that is only because God is fine-tuning your character and your destiny so that everything is perfect when the time is right. Be patient. Your promotion from your detour will arrive at the perfect time for you to fulfill your destiny.

Prayer

Lord, I want to be ready when it is time for me to fulfill my
destiny. Waiting is hard. Being broken is hard. But, God, I trust
that You are doing this for the perfection of Your purpose.
Help me to continue to trust You as I wait and thank You for
the promotion that is up ahead. In Christ's name, amen.

THE PROVIDENCE OF
DETOURS

Start

Welcome everyone to session 6 of Detours.

As you consider the impact of this study on your thinking, what was a helpful point of review or a new insight gained from your personal study in the last week?

Does anybody have a special takeaway, a story or updates related to our discussion and application from the previous group sessions?

In our final session we'll focus on the providence of detours.

Share an experience when you've had something you were dreading turn out to be something that was quite pleasant, even a blessing in your life or others.

Today, Dr. Evans explores the providence of detours and we will see how Joseph's purpose and story came full circle. What others meant for trouble, even evil, for Joseph, the Lord used for good. Often, in our own lives the Lord uses the hard parts of our lives to bring about good and revelations of His glory.

Before we see what Dr. Evans has to teach us about God's providence in detours, would somebody pray for our time together, asking the Lord to open our hearts and minds to His Word?

Watch

Complete this viewer guide as you watch the video for session 6.

You cannot have a _Sovereign God_ and _Lock_.

Providience is God stitching things together to bring them to a _Purposeful Steering End_.

God's hand is the sovereign, providential hand guiding the _Purposeful Wheel Of History_.

God has a _divinelly - Ordained Purpose_ for your life.

When God's agenda is working, God is _glorfied_, people are _destinyd_, and you are _benefited_.

God is so much in _Control_, He can use evil to achieve _his Goal Purpose_

When God releases you from your detour, you will _Popur_ because God has _Purpose_ in the pain.

Respond

Discuss the video with your group, using the questions below.

Read Genesis 50:18-21. Review the awful times and trials of Joseph's life. How did God use all of these terrible things for good?

What are some other popular words like "luck" to which we mistakenly use to refer to what is actually God's providence?

Share a time when you've mistakenly assigned luck, or a related word or phrase as the cause of a situation or change that you now understand was God's providence.

Dr. Evans defines providence as God stitching things together to bring them to a purposeful end. How does this definition change your perspective of the circumstances in your life right now?

Read Romans 8:28. In light of this scripture, and what we've read in Genesis 50:18-21, how are you comforted and encouraged by the providence of God?

Dr. Evans said, "God is so much in control, He can use evil to achieve His goal." How have you seen God use evil for good?

In our current culture, we are surrounded by evil. How does what we've studied today and in this Bible study encourage you?

If you are currently in or have recently found yourself in a detour, share with the group what you believe God has been teaching you. Be encouraged that God has purpose in your detour.

What are some key moments you will take away from your time together as a group?

Read week 6 and complete the activities to conclude your study of Detours.

God Is in Control

Providence is one of the most important things you need to know in your Christian experience. The first most important thing, of course, is the gospel. You need to know how to come to faith in Jesus Christ for your eternal destiny through the forgiveness of your sins.

But following the truth of salvation, the second most important thing you must know in your Christian life is this concept of providence. Providence is the hand of God in the glove of history.

First Timothy 6:15 reminds us that God is the ruler over all and brings everything to pass in His perfect timing. We read, "...which He will bring about at the proper time—He who is the blessed and only Sovereign, the King of kings and Lord of lords."

God's sovereignty means that He is the absolute ruler, controller, and sustainer of His creation. He is the One who has the final say. Nothing, absolutely nothing, sits outside of God's sovereignty.

There are no events over which He does not rule. There are no situations that happen which He does not either create or allow.

Your boss does not have the last say.

Your spouse does not have the last say.

Your parents do not have the last say.

Your health does not have the last say.

Even you do not have the last say.

God created this world and all that is within it—and He rules over all. This is the concept we will look at this week—the concept simply called providence.

Day 1

LUCK OF THE DRAW

Detours are disappointing. Detours are annoying. Oftentimes, detours are even confusing. Too many disappointed, annoyed, and confused people today are trying to "luck" or "positively think" their way to their destiny rather than seek what God is doing in the detour to get them there. They are hoping if they just run into enough good vibes that this will somehow bring about the life they want.

Joseph didn't visualize his way out of the prison. There is no account of him meditating his way out or even using positive affirmations to get out. The Bible doesn't tell us he sat there in jail repeating over and over again, "I am a free man. I am a free man. I am a free man." Positive thinking encourages the mind and the spirit, and it is a healthy thing to do. But when you put your faith in the basket of your own mind's power to work out your destiny, you've set yourself up as an idol.

What we read about Joseph's time in jail focuses more on God than it does on Joseph. Write out the key phrases from each passage that focuses on what God did with or for Joseph.

Genesis 39:21

1.

2.

3.

Genesis 39:23

1.

2.

It was God who got Joseph out of jail. It was God who got Joseph a job. It was God who showed restraint in moving too soon while Joseph's character was being shaped. It was God who saw the end from the beginning and orchestrated all that was necessary to take Joseph on the detours that led him straight to a destiny of epic proportions. In fact, when Stephen reviews the life of Joseph in the Book of Acts, he gives the secret of his success when he says, "Yet God was with him" (Acts 7:9).

It was God who arranged the circumstances always and ultimately in Joseph's favor. But the word we use when we refer to God's sovereign control and arrangement of life is not *luck*. It is another word—providence.

Write out your view of what providence means.

How do you compare providence to things we often describe like luck or chance?

Do you view providence as something dependent upon your own thoughts or will? Why or why not?

Providence is a word that expresses one of the key ways God demonstrates His sovereignty in connection with His intentional arrangement of people, circumstances, and events to achieve His sovereign purposes. Sovereignty is God's rule. Providence is how God uses that rule to integrate, connect, attach, detach, arrange, and hook things up to facilitate His purposes.

Read Ephesians 1:11. What do we learn about providence and God's sovereignty from this verse?

Different translations of Ephesians 1:11 use different words. Spend a moment using other Bible resources to look at the various ways this passage states this truth. Write down the different words used for the term meaning *everything.*

What do all of these different words used for the term *everything* have in common in their meaning?

This being so, what percentage of things does God work out according to His own purpose and His own will?

Scripture states fully and unmistakably that God's plans cannot be thwarted. He works out ALL things according to His will. One reality that cannot ever take place is the simultaneous existence of both sovereignty and luck. The two can never commingle. When a sovereign God exists who controls all things, you cannot also at the same time have random events (luck) that shape things. One excludes the other.

What you may feel is luck or call luck is never luck. Just like darkness cannot abide where there is light, luck cannot exist within the rule of a sovereign, providential Creator God.

Read 1 Chronicles 29:11-12. According to this passage, what part of creation and order does God rule over?

Read Job 42:2. How many plans of God can be thwarted?

Read Proverbs 19:21. Compare man's plans with God's purposes. In the end, which will stand?

Joseph's life definitely had multiple ups and downs. He is dressed in a coat of many colors one day and naked in a pit the next day. He's got a great job one day and is accused of rape the next. He is in a prison, forgotten by someone he helped one day and shaved, washed, and standing before Pharaoh in the palace the next.

Joseph's life may feel like a roller coaster on a lot of levels. If we were to use the concept of luck, it would appear that this is a man of great luck and bad luck. But what may have felt unlucky one day was actually God providentially positioning Joseph for his ultimate destiny. Remember Genesis 50:20? If you don't, go back and re-read it.

Through these words, we see that Joseph had a grasp on God's providence. God is also providentially arranging the days, events, relationships, and emotions of your life to bring you to your destiny. Trust Him. This isn't His first time.

Prayer

Faithful God, thank You for the way You weave things
together for my good. At times I don't always recognize
Your hand or the difficulties I face as a means of
moving me to where You want me to be. I release these
expectations I have of how things should be, according
to me, and choose to trust in You and Your ability to work
all things together for good. In Christ's name, amen.

Day 2

OOPS, I MISSED THAT ONE

I don't know if you are an expert in the area of geometry, trigonometry, algebra, or even fractions, but in terms of the mathematical formulas that these things represent, you can bet one thing: They all rest on one simple principle, that one plus one equals two. If you don't get the fundamentals of mathematics right as the foundation for all else, you will never be able to make sense of the more complicated things such as geometric calculations. All of the complexities of math fit firmly on the foundation of its base.

Life may feel like trigonometry sometimes. It may feel like a difficult geometric equation. Things can get so complicated that they simply don't add up, but if you start with the foundation that God is sovereign and in His sovereignty, He providentially arranges all things to accomplish His goal, then you have the foundation upon which to properly solve the complexities life sends your way.

What you, I, and others may look at as random events, chance encounters, or arbitrary connections are actually orchestrated events in both the purpose and plan of God. God is sitting behind the steering wheel of history. Sometimes He has us on the main highway.

Other times it's down a back alley. Sometimes it looks like we are going the wrong way on a one-way street. Whatever the case, God's intentions are immaculate, and His plans are providential.

Take a moment to think of a time when you felt you were off your path toward a desire, goal, or dream, and in hindsight, you see how God was working all things out for His purpose. Write about that experience and what you learned from it.

Just as not all detours occur on the major thoroughfares of life, God's providence isn't only connected to the major things that happen to us. We may recognize His hand in the big things more easily, but the Lord is intimately involved in the small things as well. Sovereignty is so complete and providence so intricate that it is delicately woven through every detail of life.

Read Matthew 10:29. What does this verse tell us about God's ultimate control over all things?

Now read Matthew 10:30. God knows how many hairs are on your head. Based on this truth, in what ways do you think God is interested in the small details of your life?

Do you think most Christians realize that God is concerned with what we call the minor things in our lives? Why or why not?

Sometimes it's easy to see the devil in the details but what would help our perspective and our responses to life would be to recognize that God is in them all the more. In fact, the devil may be bad, mean, and wanting to hurt someone, but even the devil had to ask permission before he laid a hand on Job's situation. The devil is on a leash—God's leash, under God's sovereign hand. Joseph's brothers, and even the devil, may have thought they were thwarting the vision Joseph had regarding his great position in his dream as a teen, but what was meant by them for evil was used by God for good.

Read Isaiah 46:9-10. How can you take comfort in this verse?

Read Lamentations 3:37. Our words have power (when they are in alignment with God's will). How does this verse clarify what many call the "name it and claim it" approach to life?

In what way does resting in the reality of God's sovereignty free your emotions up from worry, doubt, anxiety, and more?

Providence means God never says, "Oops, I missed that one." He doesn't say that because He is in control of all, the big things to the small, so nothing surprises Him, even though they do surprise us in our finite thinking. You can't google God's providence or plans to find out what He is going to do. You can't go to your computer and type in the words "God's ways for my life" and come up with the details of how He is doing what He plans to do with you.

God is beyond our ability to figure out. Don't be surprised when He just doesn't make sense. He is not supposed to. His ways are not our ways and His thoughts are higher than our thoughts. They are as far as the heaven is to the earth. The gap between our thinking and God's thinking is infinite. We can't figure Him out. He is the unfigure-outable God.

Read Romans 11:33. What does this verse tell us about God's ways?

Recall a time when God did not make sense in your life. Did you choose to trust Him in this situation? What was the result?

If you ever discover how to truly embrace this truth of providence, you will begin to view all of life differently. You will rest when you used to fret. You will breathe easily when you used to worry. You will give thanks when you used to be filled with bitterness or regret.

To fully live out the purpose of your destiny and maximize the paths of your detours, you must live and look at the events of your life through the windshield of providence.

Prayer

Lord, bless me with the grace to accept that You have all things in Your providential control. Give me the virtue of trust. Allow me to release my anxiety, worry, and need for control to You, since You ultimately rule over all. I honor You with my hope and my heart. In Christ's name, amen.

Day 3

CONNECTING GOD TO EVERYTHING

Many of you going through this Bible study on detours are waiting for God to do something. You are waiting for your change to come. Maybe you are in a situation in life where you are saying on a regular basis, "I didn't sign up for this."

Perhaps you didn't sign up to still be single or walked out on as a spouse and left as a single parent. Maybe you didn't sign up for a miserable relationship or to be stuck in a job that brings you no satisfaction and barely pays your bills. It could be that you are in a difficult health situation or have lost a loved one, and you are sitting there saying, "I didn't sign up for this. This is not how I wanted my life to be." Despite believing God, asking God, calling on God, and looking for God to make a move, you are still stuck wondering when you will arrive at your destiny.

If this is you, what I want you to know as a believer in Jesus Christ is this— you have a destiny. Oftentimes, you are closer than you think. Pass the test. Don't throw in the towel. Respond rightly to wrong treatment. Do good. Defend the defenseless. Honor God. Grow in faith. Trust. Wait. And before you know it, your destiny suddenly will be upon you. Yes, those things are often difficult to do, so remember this: As you meander through the detours toward your destiny of living out your divine design, the thing that will allow you to keep going despite life's circumstances is knowing that God truly is in control. God's providential hand will work it all out for good when you trust Him fully in your heart and actions.

Now, read Proverbs 16:4. Do you believe that God can even use the negative things and people in life to bring you into your destiny? Why or why not?

The secret to Joseph arriving at his destiny is that he understood and accepted the providence of God. He didn't give God the cold shoulder when things went bad for him. He remained close to the Lord, despite the darkest of days. As a result, God stayed close to him, too. While he was in the deepest pit of jail, the Lord was with Joseph.

While serving the basest of people in the prison system, God caused all that Joseph did to prosper. While living as a slave in the house of a high official, the Lord blessed Joseph's hands. Even when Joseph finally made it to stand before Pharaoh, and if ever there was a time for self-promotion in order to maneuver his way out of the dungeon, Joseph deferred to God in all things. Now, with God's track record of allowing Joseph to suffer a significant amount in his life, do you think it might have been understandable for Joseph to be shy about continuing to lean on God now that things finally started to look good?

But, he wasn't shy. Joseph immediately connected himself with God during what may have seemed like his only method of escape out of a life in prison. "It is not in me; God will give Pharaoh a favorable answer" (Gen. 41:16).

How does Joseph's commitment to God through the bad and the good encourage you in your own walk with the Lord?

Read Genesis 41:25-28. How many times does Joseph refer to God? What does this tell us about his understanding of God's power and providence?

When have you seen God with you in a dark moment in your own life? How did His providence give you comfort?

Read Isaiah 45:7. Does this verse broaden your view of God in any way? If so, in what way?

How does it shed light on God's use of detours in bringing each of us to our destinies?

If you take God seriously, you can never be a victim of your circumstances. Your circumstances wouldn't be your circumstances without God allowing them. If Satan is able to remove your consideration of God within the circumstances and direct your attention to questions, doubt, or resentment—particularly if it is a negative circumstance—he has succeeded in adding more delays to your detours.

Should Satan remove your trust and keep God out of the equation of your understanding of your circumstances in life, you will lose perspective of His providence. When you do, you will also run the risk of prolonging your detours as He continues to teach you lessons of faith and trust.

Prayer

Lord, You truly do have control over all things—even the things that don't make sense, don't feel good, or seem to be disappointments in life. I want to please You in my responses to these things. Give me a greater awareness of Your providence so that my responses to life's detours are in alignment with Your rule over all. In Christ's name, amen.

Day 4
OPENING DOORS THAT SEEMED SLAMMED SHUT

Have you ever seen God do something in your life or in someone else's life that didn't make sense? You had a door opened for you that you didn't even know to knock on? Joseph's life reveals what God does so well. He can promote you and position you into a destiny way beyond your wildest dreams.

Joseph had no credentials to get where he needed to be. He had no credentials to land him the job of saving nations from famine. He had no personal contacts, political contacts, relational contacts, or even circumstantial contacts. He could pull no strings or pave no paths. He was a nobody in a foreign land with no resume or name to assist him.

Everything that society looks for to make a person successful—Joseph had none of it. ALL Joseph had was God. But, God was more than enough to make up for everything else he lacked.

Take a look at 1 Peter 5:6. What is a key component in God lifting you up and promoting you?

What does it mean/look like to humble yourself before God?

One way Joseph humbled himself before God was through making God the sum total of his life. God was the sum total of the why, what, and how in Joseph's world. We know this because all through his story, God was referenced no matter what the circumstances were.

God was to Joseph what the ocean is to a pebble in it—the ocean totally encompasses the pebble just as God completely enveloped Joseph's life. We also ought to acknowledge God as totally surrounding us.

When you are overwhelmed by your circumstances, fill yourself completely and consolingly with God. The thing that marked Joseph apart from so many others was that his was a life punctuated by God's presence.

Read Psalm 75:6-7. Why is it good to trust in God, rather than yourself or others, to get you to the place of fully living out your purpose?

Read Daniel 2:21. How much power do people really have over their own promotions?

In what way does this truth give you comfort or conviction?

It seems that we live in a society where so much emphasis is put on striving after what culture says you must have, be, and do in order to climb the ladder of success and influence. Society tells us we need to pile on our degrees, network, look a certain way, say or do certain things to get somewhere in life—but look at Joseph. The man was stripped of every single thing a man can be stripped of, except for one thing: his destiny. Because his destiny sat securely in the hand of God.

You, too, can reach the pinnacle of your purpose. You don't have to climb there alone. God has a million ways of opening doors, re-directing paths, and getting you right where you need to be.

Read Luke 14:11. What is the most important thing you can and should be doing while waiting on God to open doors for you?

Detours

What are some ways the Lord seeks to cultivate humility in each of us?

Is there something you need to surrender to God that you have taken too much pride in? In what way can you surrender this?

When your destiny is in God's hands and you are trusting God with all your heart—in spite of your circumstances, mistakes, detours, and distractions—no one can block what God has for you. You may have lost a lot in your life, but you have not lost your destiny.

If you will simply align your perspective with the Lord's, you may be closer to reaching your destiny than you think.

God loves to turn things on a dime. He loves to operate in the surprise of the suddenlies. When He does, He is the only One who can get the credit and the glory.

Read Matthew 5:16. Who is to get the glory for the good things you do?

Is there an area in your life where you are seeking the glory and the credit? What tangible action can you take to reverse your approach in this situation or area of your life?

Read Psalm 115:1. How can you make this verse a central part of your worldview and life choices, including what you say and what you share on social media or with others?

Perspective is key in going through your detours, particularly with regard to God's providence. Perspective is how you choose to view something. It's like the boy who lost his contact lens and was looking for it for thirty minutes. He couldn't locate it even after all that time. His mom walked in the room and asked him what he was doing.

Within a minute of looking for the contact lens, his mom had found it. "How did you find it so quickly?" the boy asked.

"We weren't looking for the same thing," his mom replied. "You were looking for a contact lens. I was looking for $150." Big difference. And it's found in perspective.

It is critical to have the right perspective on God's providential hand while pursuing your destiny—particularly when you are on a detour. When you are in that place where you have not yet hit your sweet spot, you need to know how to view things with trust, faith, and hope. You may feel far removed from purpose, passion, and peace, but sometimes you are only a step away. God can change things when it's time—in an instant.

Prayer

Lord, I want to have the right perspective on Your providential hand in my life. I want to rest in Your control. Thank You for teaching me these important principles as I seek to make my life model that of Christ. You are in charge and You know what You are doing. I trust You in all things, Lord. In Christ's name, amen.

Day 5
ARRIVING AT YOUR DESTINATION

Everyone seems to want their blessing. Everyone seems to want their destiny. But few seem to want the development it takes to get there. Understanding and embracing providence is also found in understanding and embracing God's intentional development in our lives.

A kid will eat candy all day long. He or she will play games and spend your money all day long, yet candy, games, and money won't develop a child into becoming a productive adult. Give them correction, discipline—guidance that goes against what they want—and they will often complain, or even disobey.

God knows the same holds true for us. In order for God to have Joseph fulfill his role as second in command in Egypt, He had to take him deeper first. He had to develop him first. He had to strengthen his humility, trust, confidence (as opposed to pride), and leadership skills. He also gave him lessons on dealing with accusers and haters along the way, since a position of prominence would no doubt attract the same.

Read Philippians 2:13. In what ways does God often work "in" you in order to direct desires, sharpen skills, or develop your character?

Are you experiencing God working "in" you at this time? How have these lessons on detours and providence helped put this in perspective?

According to Ecclesiastes 7:13-14 and Job 12:13-16, name four things God does that no one can change or stop.

1.

2.

3.

4.

Understanding that all things are providentially controlled by God is one of the greatest ways to give you the right perspective in life. Yes, God even allows the negative things in our lives to sharpen us, motivate us, and humble us. It's like the army captain who had soldiers in training and asked them all to jump over the riverbed. The goal was to get over the river and land on the other side. All of the men and women jumped but none of them made it. Some made it halfway. Others made it two-thirds, but not one person made it over.

That's when the army captain let loose an alligator in the river and asked them to try again. This time, all of them made it. Apparently a bit of negative motivation pushed them farther than they would have gone on their own.

Sometimes you need to learn your lessons to pass the test. You need to experience the consequences of poor choices. You need to mature, focus, and eliminate outside distractions. It would be nice if we were all born wise and motivated, but we aren't. Thus, God allows and sometimes even orchestrates lessons in our lives to shape us into who He wants us to be in order to live out our destinies.

Read Matthew 28:18. In what way does Christ's authority over all help you to trust Him more in the negative realities of life?

All of this talk on providence may lead you to believe that you have little control or options in your life. This couldn't be further from the truth. The best way I know how to explain it is by using my favorite sport to both have played and now to watch: football. In football, there are sidelines and goal lines which serve as sovereign boundaries. These do not move. You can't negotiate them. You can't make them wider or more narrow. These are fixed standards with which the game of football is played. If you step over a sideline, you are out of bounds. Period. Because that is a boundary.

Within those boundaries, teams are free to run their own plays. They can call a good play or a bad play. They can gain yardage or they can lose ground. They are free to play within the boundaries established by the game.

God is sovereign in the boundaries He has set for us. But even in His providence, He allows freedom within those boundaries which give us the choice to do good or to do bad. To be right or to be wrong. To intend evil or to intend good.

While freedom doesn't cause evil, it does allow for it. That is not saying He endorses evil or sin, but rather He redeems it. He redeems the bad intention of someone who may have hurt you on purpose by intervening in you to twist that thing to work for your good. He can even redeem the bad you have done if you will surrender to Him in humility. His merciful hand will use what was meant for harm and turn it around for good, as we have seen with Joseph.

Re-write the following verse, summarizing it in your own words:

Genesis 50:20

Since God is sovereign, nothing happens outside of His rule. But within His rule, He has created freedom. Freedom means you get to choose. There is no freedom without choice. You are free to say "yes" or to say "no." You are free to go or you are free to stay. God created freedom. You are free to delay your own detour longer than necessary, and you are also free to help usher in its completion.

In light of all that has been studied and looked at in this Bible study, what are some things you can do or attitude and heart changes you can make to best align yourself with God?

Through Joseph's life story, we are reminded of this very important principle: The negative things in life do not have to lead to a negative outcome. Joseph's brothers meant evil, and with the very evil they used, God used those crimes for good.

Providence includes using the negative to produce a positive. God's sovereignty also includes the bad and what other people mean for harm. Or even the mistakes you have made in your past.

In what way does this truth help you face difficult people or situations with a more God-honoring spirit?

It's probably a verse you have heard so many times that it may have somehow lost its impact, but if you will let the truth to sink in, it can change your entire life:

And we know that God causes all things to work together for good to those who love God, to those who are called according to His purpose.
ROMANS 8:28

That good will always be connected with conforming you to the image of Christ (Rom. 8:29). To that end, He will use all things to work together for your good.

Prayer

Lord, I love you. Thank you for the power of Your purpose. Thank You for the promise of working all things together for good. I humbly bow before you on these detours in my life, asking for Your presence and favor to consistently be with me along the way. I leave the outcome in Your hands, where it belongs. I focus on serving You today, honoring You in my decisions, words and thoughts. I love You, Lord. In Christ's name, amen.

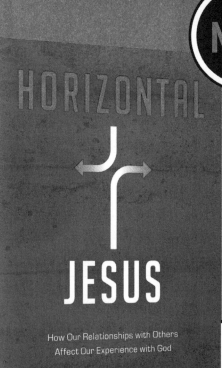

At The Urban Alternative, the national ministry of Dr. Tony Evans, we seek to restore hope and transform lives to reflect the values of the kingdom of God. Along with our community outreach initiative, leadership training and family and person growth emphasis, Dr. Evans continues to minister to people from the pulpit to the heart as the relevant expositor with the powerful voice. Lives are touched both locally and abroad through our daily radio broadcast, weekly television ministry and internet platform.

Presenting an
ALTERNATIVE to:

Community Outreach

Equipping leaders to engage public schools and communities with mentoring, family support services and a commitment to a brighter tomorrow.

Leadership Training

Offering an exclusive opportunity for pastors and their wives to receive discipleship from Drs. Tony & Lois Evans and the TUA staff, along with networking opportunities, resources and encouragement.

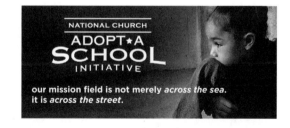

Family and Personal Growth

Strengthening homes and deepening spiritual lives through helpful resources that promote hope and health for the glory of God.

TonyEvans.org

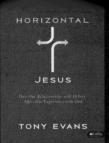

WHERE TO GO FROM HERE

Now that you've completed this study, here are a few possible directions you can go for your next one.

PARENTING

CULTURE

PRAYER

Plumb the Bible's wisdom about parenting, discipline, the role of the church, and shaping a child's heart toward the gospel. (7 sessions)

Achieve a better understanding and approach to prayer through the prayers of Paul. (8 sessions)

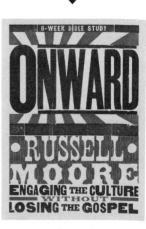

Learn to reclaim the distinctiveness of the Christian faith that sets it apart from the surrounding culture. (6 sessions)